INSPIRED

BY

COUNTRY

an artist's journey
back to nature

landscape painting

with gouache

Marji Hill

The Prison Tree Press

Published by The Prison Tree Press 2021

Suite 124

1-10 Albert Avenue

Broadbeach, Queensland 4218

Copyright © 2021 Marji Hill

Copyright © 2021 Artwork by Marji Hill

Paperback ISBN: 9780992411879

EBook ISBN: 9780992411886

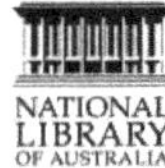 A catalogue record for this work is available from the National Library of Australia

Editor: Eddie Dowd

Poem reprinted with the permission of Eddie Dowd

https://marjihill.com

https://www.fastselfpublishing.com

ACKNOWLEDGEMENTS

In the spirit of reconciliation, I acknowledge the Traditional Custodians of Country throughout Australia and their connections to land, sea, and community. I pay my respect to elders, past, present, and emerging and extend my respect to all Aboriginal and Torres Strait Islander peoples today.

As a resident of the Gold Coast, I pay my respects to the people of the Yugambeh language region of the Gold Coast and all their descendants both past and present.

In the spirit of reconciliation, my mission is to increase the understanding between Indigenous and Non-Indigenous Australians and to provide people from all over the globe some basic understanding of Australia's first people, their history, and cultures.

My appreciation also for the support from Sherien Foley and Mary Hartstein who accompanied me into the hinterland on my painting expeditions.

DEDICATION

To

Sherien Foley

Our Faerie Queen

TABLE OF CONTENTS

1. Painting Outdoors 1

2. Painting Country 11

3. Australia's Religious Art Tradition 15

4. An Art of Antiquity 19

5. My Place 35

6. Let's Paint 49

7. Painting with Gouache 71

8. How to Paint Outdoors 85

About Marji Hill 107

Resources 113

More Books by Marji Hill 117

Chapter 1

Painting Outdoors

Painting Country and deriving inspiration from it is a rewarding, artistic experience which can be full of joy, a healing experience, and adventure.

Painting is a way of creating a meditative space. It is mindfulness at its best and allows us to escape out of our usual world.

Painting helps us to centre ourselves, and we are taken into a realm that is both calm and focussed.

When we paint Country we contemplate its beauty; we have an in-depth experience that takes us into our inner world. This stimulates our emotions, opening fresh ways of thinking, going about our life, and simply being.

Let's go on a journey together and…

- venture beyond the walls of our home,

- take a trip into the countryside, into the lands of ancient Australia,

- soak up the experience,

- see how the colour and light creates mood and atmosphere,

- have an emotional response to what we see,

- be inspired and excited by what's in front of us,

- appreciate the antiquity of the landscape

- perhaps it is Country that provokes a challenging response to a land not to our liking?

- remnants of extinct volcanic activity that happened millions of years ago?

- desert land expanding forever beyond the horizon?

- being in the lands of another culture? and,

- feeling the spirit of that Country.

Our response to Country can happen at a multitude of levels.

This book is for those who want to draw on their creativity, who are inspired by Country, and who want to paint Country.

The experience of painting Country goes beyond a visual response. It may provoke a deeper response encompassing historical, spiritual and cultural elements with deeper layers of meaning.

All of this impacts the artist's psyche, how to intuitively respond through paint in their depiction of what they see before them.

In the pages that follow I take you on a journey sharing with you an artistic experience.

It's a journey into the Australian countryside set within the context of Australia's ancient history and traditions.

It's about learning to paint in the Australian open air

It's about painting our response to Country

It's about how we perceive that Country

It's about learning to paint with the most amazingly versatile medium – gouache.

Part of this journey will involve digging deep into Australia's past with a snapshot of how Australia's First People responded to their land and how they expressed their response in art, paint, and ceremony.

This expression of art and understanding what Country means impacts an artist's perception of Country and how to go about painting it.

Painting in the landscape and being inspired by Country, is deeply embedded into the Australian artistic psyche.

After we delve into Australia's artistic antiquity and its traditions we journey into a specific part of Australia that is imbued with these many layers of meaning. We visit, are inspired, and paint in the Springbrook National Park which is part of the Gondwana Rainforests of Australia World Heritage Area.

Springbrook encompasses it all.

Springbrook is Country…

- full of ancient history and culture

- in which traditional custodians carefully implemented land management practices

- used its rich natural resources for thousands of years

- containing sacred places and sites of special significance

- with contours that have been shaped and moulded by ancient volcanoes and erosion

- Country which is a remnant of a once huge shield volcano that dominated the region about 23 million years ago

- that dominates the western skyline of Queensland's Gold Coast, with its lush rain forests, cascading waterfalls, and mountain streams

- is Country that offers impressive vistas with its subtropical and temperate rainforest

Following this introduction to meaning in Australian Country and to a place where artists can be inspired to paint, they are introduced to the basics of painting outdoors and to how they can combine this with completing their artworks back in the studio.

You will also get an overview of the necessary tool kit for painting outdoors, the materials needed, and the selection of subject matter.

Master the art of painting a compelling outdoor composition using the subtleties of gouache water colour paint to create beautifully expressive subjects and themes.

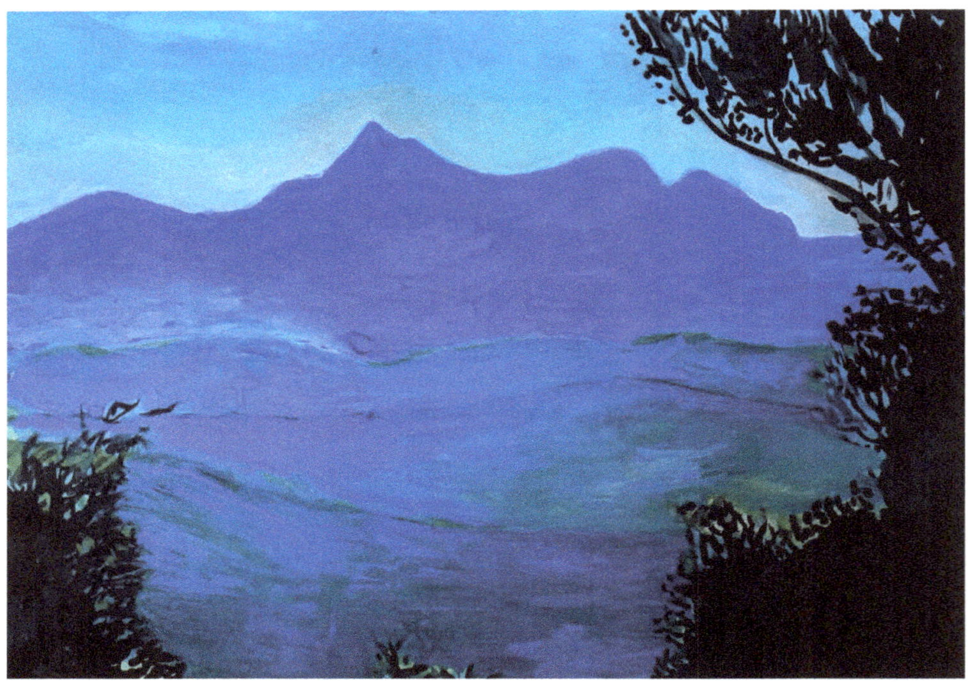

A Sculptured Country

This is an opportunity to explore a daring and expressive medium - painting with gouache - and taking an artistic journey into the world of the Springbrook National Park.

Be ready to…

- rejuvenate the mind and soul,

- be inspired by spectacular vistas,

- engage the senses,

- soak up the unique experience of painting in the open air,

- tap into the emotional and psychological health benefits of painting,

- its effect on the spirit as one goes back to nature, and,

- benefit from the meditative experience, another way of practising mindfulness and being in the present.

I was introduced to the value of painting outdoors many years ago when a friend, Mike Parr, a distinguished Australian performance artist and print maker said to me — go out and paint in the landscape. It will strengthen your powers of observation, you will see the subtleties of colour, you will benefit from painting in the landscape.

Painting away from the home in the open air is called *plein air* painting. It will:

- enhance an artist's perception,

- improve their powers of observation,

- experience the light, its forever changing and ephemeral qualities,

- capture colours, and the changing details of weather and light,

- a rewarding experience,

- a powerful experience, together with its

- spontaneity and freshness

Painting outside is a marvellous escape out of the comfort zone which pushes the boundaries as one learns to respond quickly and to paint just as rapidly.

Getting outside to paint is even more beneficial than it would have been in the time of the early Impressionists. It offers time away from the indoors allowing us to experience things that we would otherwise may not have been able to do.

Plein air painting fits well into the Australian way - the love of the Australian bush, the desire to be outdoors, and being able to go back to nature.

With the addition of photography, capture aspects of the landscape, its detail, gain clarity of a certain shape or texture, and bring all of this data home to create your masterpiece.

Painting outside is not without its challenges. The light can change swiftly and weather conditions suddenly change. Experience intense heat, or extreme cold, and there is nothing worse than wind.

Also, how annoying are the insects - the flies, ants, and bugs. And, of course, be ready for that stream of onlookers.

There are issues with the type of paint artists use: acrylic paint can get hard as it dries fast in hot, dry conditions and cannot be reused; oil paint, by contrast, takes a long time to dry.

Be ready to be inspired by Country. Gain an understanding of how painting in Country is part of an

incredible Australian tradition that dates back at least
65,000 years, if not more.

As we go into my favourite part of the world, the
Springbrook National Park, be introduced to gouache
water colour painting, its history, its qualities, its
versatility, and learn its application as an expressive *plein
air* artistic medium.

Chapter 2

Painting Country

Painting outdoors, painting Country, belongs to an ancient tradition in Australia.

Making art in the land is a major constituent of the Australian Indigenous cultural tradition. It has an antiquity - 65,000 years- and probably more.

It shares a history. Painting outside in the country in the European tradition is called *en plein air*.

In the decades following 1788 Australian colonial artists such as John Glover and Eugene von Guérard, began to paint the land of their new island continent. They created artwork in preparation for paintings that were completed in the studio.

In the non-Indigenous Australian context *plein air* painting became associated with Australian

Impressionism with artists such as Tom Roberts, Arthur Streeton, Charles Conder, Jane Sutherland, Clara Southern, Frederick McCubbin and Jane Price.

What is regarded as an Australian school of art and sometimes known as Australia's "first" school has to be reconsidered within Australia's ancient history of art.

We have to acknowledge that in this country, Australia does have a shared history of art. There is a great tradition of art making.

Australia's first people made art enriched by their innate connection to and knowledge of Country. Then there was the art introduced to this country by the British colonialists.

The phrase *en plein air* was coined by the French and it means painting outside the home in the landscape. The painter leaves the walls of the home and studio and goes outside into the open air to paint.

"Outside" could be the immediate environment of the home. It can mean painting in the garden, painting out in the park, or by the sea, in the mountains, in the countryside, or out in the desert.

In the European tradition the practice of going out into the landscape to paint goes back centuries, possibly as old as art itself, but it became an art form created by the French Impressionists. More than any other art movement, Impressionism became synonymous with *plein air* or 'open air' painting.

In the 1800s *plein air* painting was very popular largely because of the invention not only of metal paint tubes but a special type of easel. These inventions meant artists could then move around in the countryside more freely.

Artists like Claude Monet, Pierre-Auguste Renoir, Alfred Sisley and Frédéric Bazille, in the 1860s ventured into the countryside and discovered that they could paint in sunlight directly from nature. These painters would try to capture the natural light and to depict in paint the forever changing and ephemeral qualities of the light.

The Australian Impressionist painters were influenced by the art that was being made in France but the paintings made in this side of the world had a distinctive Australian flavour.

When Tom Roberts returned to Australia from Europe in 1885 and set up an artists' camp outside the city

Melbourne the concept of *plein air* painting gathered momentum in Australia.

Australian painters from the European tradition ventured into the countryside and painted their response to and their perception of the environment around them.

The challenge of trying to capture the ever-changing qualities of light and atmosphere characterised this art movement.

Chapter 3

Australia's Religious Art Tradition

In the nineteenth century Australian Impressionist painters were influenced by art that was being made in France but the paintings took on a distinctive Australian character.

In contrast to the French Impressionists, and the European tradition, visual representations of Country had been going on in Australia for probably much longer than 65,000 years.

In the spirit of reconciliation my mission is to increase the understanding between Indigenous and Non-Indigenous Australians and to provide people from all over the globe some basic understanding of Australia's first people, its history and cultures.

Within this framework then I show how Australian Aboriginal art has continued from its earliest beginnings to the present day enriched by a religious, innate connection to and knowledge of land.

Art has been made outside in the country for many centuries even following the devastating changes to Australian Indigenous cultures following 1788.

The ancient traditions of Aboriginal art stem from a different perspective to that of the European art. Art making in Australia was made in the context of religious ceremony.

It was a religious expression and its production was tied to ceremony. A design on the ground, on a body, on a sculpture, or the image on the wall of a rock shelter were manifestations of the Dreamtime and connected to some ancestral Dreamtime saga.

The image of a kangaroo on a rock wall may be the Kangaroo Ancestral Hero while the geometric, abstract designs on a bark painting could tell the story of a Dreamtime creative event. Concentric circles or a "U" shape in the design of a desert ground painting connect the maker and the viewer to an ancestral episode.

Traditional Aboriginal art was part of ceremonial ritual and was an expression of a major story or song cycle. The aim of a ceremony was to evoke the power of an ancestral being and to encourage it to release again its creative powers.

The artist experienced a transcendental connection between the power that comes from making an artwork and the power that an artist feels from being part of one of the great song cycles.

A creative saga was and was re-enacted in song, dance and art. Days could be spent in preparation for a ceremony making carvings, paintings, sand sculptures and other ritual items.

Not only does traditional art tell the stories of the Dreamtime but it provides that spiritual association between human beings and the supernatural powers and links them to particular sites in Country.

Because the creation of art is a form of religious expression the act of making it put its creators into direct communication with ancestral beings enabling them to tap into ancestral power. This creative process reactivates spiritual powers and brings the artists into a relationship enabling the power to be tapped.

But to do this the artist can only ever paint or carve those designs and images that are relevant to him or her in a spiritual sense. There has to be a special totemic connection between the artist, the ancestral being and the artwork being made.

Of course, this form of art making is very different to the European concept of *plein air* painting.

Like *plein air*, however, the act of painting takes place in the open air but its creation is an expression of very deep religious faith.

Chapter 4

An Art of Antiquity

Australia is the earliest centre of civilisation in the world that continues to the present day.

Madjedbebe (formerly known as Malakunanja II) is a sandstone rock shelter in the Northern Territory. Archaeological evidence from this site indicates that human beings occupied this region over 55,000 years ago.

Archaeologists suggest that the rock shelter was probably in use around 65,000 years ago.

Mungo Man

At Lake Mungo in the Lake Mungo National Park in New South Wales evidence from a male skeleton found in 1974, revealed that this man, named Mungo Man, lived there 40,000 years ago.

Red ochre was found on his skeleton. This red ochre indicates that there must have been some form of ritual practiced at the time.

Pigments such as ochre can tell us a lot about history. Not only does the ochre found on the skeletons show that there was some form of religious ritual going on all those centuries ago but it implies that it was used for making art - in cave painting, decoration of objects, and body painting.

So, what was happening in the context of art making and religion over 40,000 years ago still happens today.

While painting on rock ended about 2000 years ago in Europe the tradition of rock painting in Australia has continued to the present day, particularly at religious art sites like in Arnhem Land in the Northern Territory, or the Kimberley in Western Australia.

Rock art in the Kimberley, northwest of Western Australia, is well known for its mimi-like stick Bradshaw figures and the Wandjina spirits. Wandjinas are huge spirit beings, almost human in form, with large headdresses.

These Wandjina spirit beings are believed to be the clouds which form before the oncoming of the wet. They are very powerful and so powerful that people even today still approach a Wandjina site with great reverence and respect.

They call out to the spirit to let it know that they are coming and to assure the Wandjina that they will do no harm to its paintings.

Quinkins

Thousands of rock shelters containing paintings and engravings are located near Laura on Cape York Peninsula in North Queensland. The key spirit figures of this art work are the Quinkins which are usually painted in one colour, particularly red.

Quicken spirits are everywhere not only as images on the rock but they are living in the cracks of rocks. They come out to frighten people and to punish people if they have been offended.

Mimi and X-ray

Another major rock art area in Australia is in the Arnhem Land escarpment.

This art is characterised by the Mimi stick like figures and the more recent X-ray paintings. Many rock art sites in Arnhem Land are sacred and cannot be visited by uninitiated people.

However, there are some that can be visited like Obiri Rock (Ubir) in Kakadu National Park.

Full of mystery these Mimi spirit figures found in caves and rock shelters are depicted dancing, fighting, hunting and carrying the dead.

X-ray paintings are said to be a more recent art than the Mimi and which overlay the earlier art are images of totemic beings - animals, birds, reptiles and fish - and which show their internal organs.

The images in Western Arnhem Land bark paintings are commonly set against a background colour like red ochre, or white, or yellow or black. They are heavily decorated and may be divided into sections but not filling the whole board.

Abstract and geometric designs are more typical of eastern Arnhem Land art styles.

Desert art

In the desert regions of Australia art was ephemeral. Drawings and art works were made on the ground and then they were either quickly erased or were left to be blown away by the wind.

A European viewer of desert art will see what appears to be abstract and geometrical designs with spirals, lines, circles and points.

But to the desert eye the designs represent the land. Just think what the country looks like to a bird flying overhead. Looking down a campsite would appear circular, as does a well, a rock or a hill.

A horseshoe design could be a person sitting or it could represent a windbreak.

Desert designs made by the men of the central desert are Dreaming tracks. These were pathways along which great ancestral heroes journeyed having their adventures.

Traditional ceremonies embodying the great song cycles were about language, song, dance and art. Much of it was secret and sacred and therefore not visible to outsiders. At the same time, some of the significant parts of it were open to all.

Traditional ceremony incorporated art, song and dance. In ceremonial preparation participants would sing, intone songs which related to the interconnected series of creative journeys and ancestral episodes making the world as we know it today.

This Dreamtime world continues even today to be all encompassing and permeating the lives of people.

Aboriginal art in the desert regions of Australia focuses on one particular tract of land. While the story may involve many very important sites for a language group painters would just focus on the specific story that is connected to their family.

Desert artists use the same symbols in their art works. Once you are familiar with the symbols and what they mean it is possible to understand the desert designs.

But these symbols may have different layers of meaning and can mean different things depending on where they are positioned to other symbols used in the paintings.

Albert Namatjira

Breaking away from this long and ancient tradition was Albert Namatjira (1902-1959). He was the first celebrated Indigenous Australian artist to gain national and international recognition.

Namatjira's paintings were created in a European style and they captured the uniqueness and grandeur of the Central Australian landscape.

Namatjira was a Western Arrernte-speaking artist from the MacDonnell Ranges in Central Australia.

He was born at Hermannsburg, at the time a Lutheran Mission and it was situated on the Finke River within the rolling, sensationally beautiful hills of the MacDonnell Ranges.

Ghost gums characterised the landscape with their amazing white trunks. Palms grew in the gorges and the mountain ranges kept changing colour from red to purple a great inspiration for artists.

In 1934, Namatjira saw an exhibition of watercolour paintings of Ntaria (the Arrente name for Hermannsburg) by European artist, Rex Battarbee and his fellow artist, John Gardner.

Seeing these paintings was to change Albert Namatjira's life.

He started experimenting with water colours and became determined to become a master water colourist in the European tradition.

In 1936 Namatjira learnt to paint the landscape under the mentorship of Rex Battarbee.

They came to an agreement. Namatjira would take Battarbee on a big painting expedition and would drive the camels. In return Battarbee would teach Namatjira to paint.

Namatjia quickly mastered the art of water colour painting. He eventually accompanied Battarbee on many expeditions accompanying him as a fellow painter.

While Namatjira was educated by the Lutherans, he was still brought up in the traditions of his culture. He was taught about his traditional Country, his language, his place in the Arrente kinship system, and how to live on and care for the land.

At the age of thirteen Namatjira went through his male initiation and he was given his Arrente name, Tonanga. He took part in the male initiation rites and religious ceremonies of his people.

In time he became a senior man and held the knowledge of his Arrente traditions with the responsibility of preserving these and handing them on to future generations.

Namatjira learnt to paint the Dreamtime stories of his people. These were the Dreamtime stories which told of the adventures and travels of the great ancestral heroes who left their tracks embedded in the landscape.

But while Namatjira was mentally steeped in ancient lore he drew on European traditions of painting. He painted in the landscape and became a master of *plein air* capturing the uniqueness and grandeur of the Central Australian landscape.

Contemporary Art Movement

A renaissance of Aboriginal art happened in the mid 1970s.

An outstanding contemporary art movement emerged developing into a fine art tradition just as genuine as the art that was made prior to European contact.

Drawing on ancient cultural and religious traditions Desert people created art works incorporating the great heroic ancestral sagas forming a new kind of contemporary art.

Its content was spiritual and religious and it was something that Western viewers could respond to even if they didn't understand the full cultural significance or the story the art was depicting.

This desert art was motivated by religious reasons but now there was a shift in that motivation.

This new style of art making gave artists an economic base in a capitalist world. It was a way of making money.

The renaissance of Indigenous art in the 1970s had its origins in traditional ground paintings.

In 1971 European art teacher, Geoffrey Bardon, at Papanya wanted a mural painted onto a wall of the school building.

He set his students to work on painting the mural. Then the senior men took over because they were concerned that the boys were attempting to paint desert stories which did not belong to them.

Firstly, they had to agree that the designs put on the wall could be viewed by everyone - men, women and children.

Finally, one of the elders, Old Tom Onion Tjapangati, gave permission for them to paint the Honey Ant Dreaming which he owned.

What was to unfold was a fervent of artistic activity with artists painting their designs on anything and everything.

This was a watershed in the history of Australian Aboriginal art.

Painting on board and then on canvas using acrylic paints became the new way. It was not long before the central Australian artists started selling their works of art and then by the late 1980s these paintings were selling for thousands of dollars.

This art movement which started as a ceremonial and religious art transformed into a secular art becoming investment art in the western world and very big industry.

Art and land ownership

Aboriginal art that was originally motivated for religious reasons was used in some circumstances to make political statements in a changing world that was dominated by Western culture.

In 1963 the Yirrkala people of North East Arnhem Land presented their bark petition to the Australian Parliament - the House of Representatives in Canberra.

Using clan designs, the petition shows all the areas of Country that were under threat from mining. These designs represented the Yirrkala title to land.

In 1976 the Australian Government passed a new law which made it possible for Aboriginal people in the Northern Territory to claim land that they could prove they traditionally owned. The designs in artwork became their title to land.

In 1978 the Anmatyerre and the Alyawarra people used their ancient stories and designs to prove that they were the traditional owners of an area called Utopia, northeast of Alice Springs.

The paintings made by the Spinifex People (Anangu Tjuta Pila Nguru) of the Great Victoria Desert are a fine example of art being used for political purposes and proving title to land. While art could help clan members claim title to land and had political implications relevant to the modern world it was still an art which was based on the fundamental principles of a long and ancient religious tradition.

Meaning in Country

A Non-Indigenous artist painting outside in County is face to face with an Australian landscape steeped in ancient history and traditions.

- painting in Country was immersed in great antiquity,

- painting was an expression of religious faith and ritual,

- painting in Country was made on the ground, on rock, on bark, in ceremonial designs on bodies, on carvings and on sculpture,

- painting was done in the open air,

- painting in Country evolved into a major world contemporary art movement.

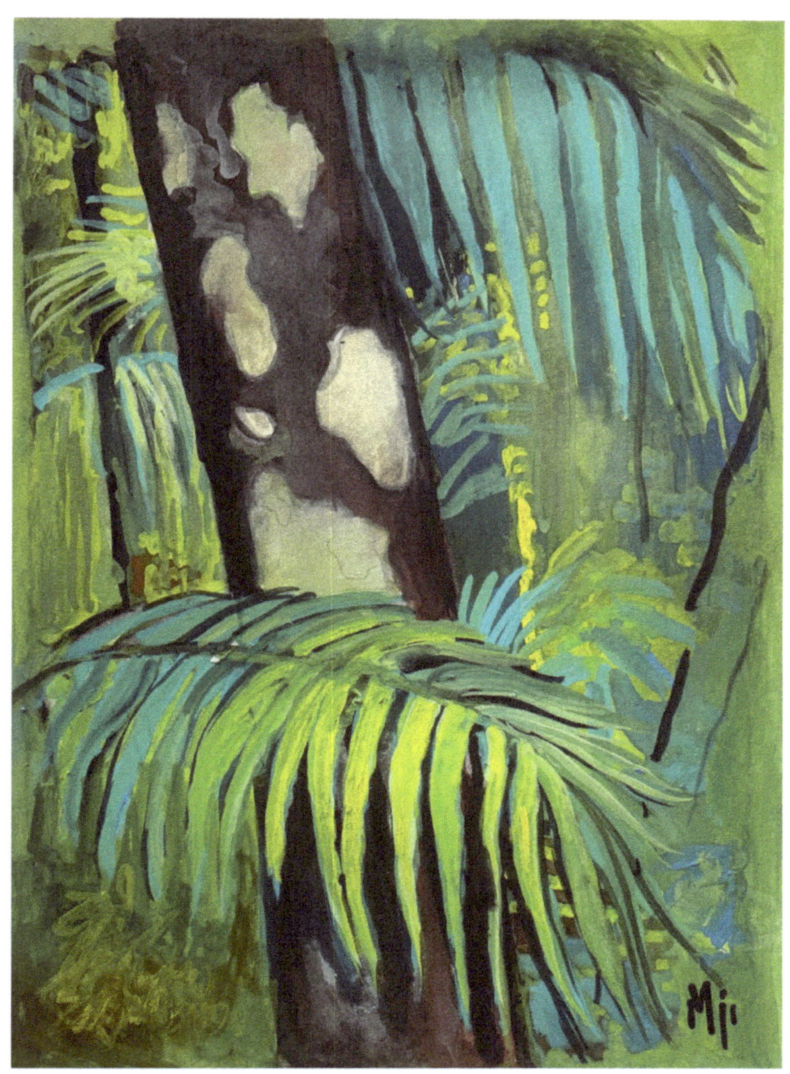

Rainforest Linking Back to Past Millennia

Chapter 5

My Place

Against this backdrop, this long and ancient tradition of art making in Country, I introduce My Place. This is an artistic journey into Country, a land full of inspiration.

In the previous chapter I presented an overview of Aboriginal art and its antiquity. This is because as I said earlier, my mission is to increase understanding between Indigenous and Non-Indigenous Australians.

Given my theme is about art making in Country, creating it beyond the walls of the home, and then bringing that creation inspired by Country back into the studio, I believe it is important to put this in the context of our long and ancient Australian artistic tradition.

An artist whose origins stem from the Anglo-Celtic or European or indeed from any other non-Aboriginal background goes into the Australian countryside to observe, to view and to respond pictorially to what they can see in front of them.

As I journey to My Place, I present a pageant demonstrating how at this one place an artist can be impacted from a variety of perspectives.

When I first went to Canberra some decades ago I distinctly remember the first impressions I had of Country around the Australian Capital Territory.

I had come from southeast Queensland a rich, vibrant, green, and sub-tropical environment. In contrast the Canberra countryside was a shock to the system.

Here was Country that appeared brown, grey and dreary. Initially, I hated it. It made me feel uncomfortable and my response was indeed negative.

I felt this way for several years until I made a new, artist friend who loved the Country of this region. He taught me to see this Country differently.

I began to observe the Canberra countryside in all its subtleties of colour variation. What appeared grey initially was in fact a myriad of subtle colours.

I began to see this country with its thousands of colour variations, a multitude of colour, and different textures. The country surrounding Canberra was taking on a whole new and fresh perspective.

I began seeing this County influenced by a new and fresh mindset.

At the time I was doing a postgraduate program at the Australian National University and I specialised in Aboriginal studies. Not only that I had been working as a Research Fellow in Education at the Australian Institute of Aboriginal and Torres Strait Islander Studies (AIATSIS).

My view of Country was undergoing a transformation.

My mindset was becoming Aboriginalised. My thinking was moving beyond the Anglo sphere to a mindset that had a heightened awareness of the meaning of Land in this country.

It was not just learning about Aboriginal culture it was learning through Aboriginal culture, embedding Aboriginal perspectives into the psyche, and developing awareness of and acknowledgement of the traditional custodians and their long and continuing relationship with Country.

It was a recognition of the Law of the Dreamtime — that all-encompassing, all-pervasive force in the lives of people, that sacred time when creation continues even today.

That time forever present when all of life is traced back to the Ancestral heroes who, as they transversed the countryside, made the rivers, the mountains, the rocks, the animals, and plants and all the features of the natural environment.

My thinking was in the process of being transformed.

I'm introducing you to My Place because My Place is very special to me. My mother always told me that this is where I was conceived. I guess she would have known.

Given this, I've grown up always having a very special even spiritual connection to My Place.

I've made many pilgrimages to My Place as a child, as a teenager, as a young woman, and now.

My Place is the Springbrook National Park.

Let's do some art-making at Springbrook.

Springbrook

As already mentioned, Springbrook National Park is part of the Gondwana Rainforests of Australia World Heritage Area. If you look west from Queensland's Gold Coast coastal strip, you'll see the mountain range, the hinterland that is the backdrop to the Gold Coast.

You don't have to venture far to visit Springbrook. It's less than an hour's drive from Surfers Paradise.

An ancient world

Some 500–550 million years ago there was an ancient super continent, called Gondwana. One hundred and eighty million years ago, this super continent started to disintegrate and Australia became a fragment of this.

Rainforests covered most of Gondwana and still today, the Gondwana Rainforests of Australia with its plants and animals are a living link not only to Australia's past but to its future evolution.

These rainforests which incorporate the Springbrook National Park connect you to a world of great antiquity.

Springbrook is home to a unique ecological and magical environment of ancient fern families, cycad and conifer species, diverse tree species and animals like the Chelidae turtles, leaf-tailed geckoes and angle-headed dragons.

These species link back to the days of the dinosaurs in past millennia.

Being here and absorbing the crystal clean, fresh mountain air is like going back in time to the early days of evolution.

The contours seen today in this World Heritage Area were shaped by molten lava from the massive Tweed volcano which was active some 23 million years ago. Then about 10 million years ago the volcano began to die.

Volcanic activity extending from Springbrook to the Lamington plateau and the Tweed Range sculptured the landscape. In the process the magnificent, classic erosion caldera landform of Wollumbin (commonly known as Mount Warning) was created. This deeply sacred mountain was the volcano's epicentre.

The country formed by the volcano was built up of highly mobile basalt lavas. It was about 80 kilometres across and 2,000 metres high.

Lava spilled in every direction for up to 100 kilometres and when it cooled it became the rocks and high plateau areas typical of the region.

This Tweed volcano is regarded as possibly the best-preserved erosion caldera in the world.

This once volcanic region can be viewed from the Best of All Lookout high up at Springbrook. A 15-minute walk from the Repeater Station along a carefully graded track brings you to the lookout where you can see Wollumbin, the remnant of that extinct volcano from a by-gone era.

300 metres along the track are the rare Antarctic Beech Trees (*Nothofagus morei)* which grow only in a few places in Australia. These trees, estimated to be about 2000 years, are living relics of the past antiquity.

At their base where the soil has been worn away over centuries are twisted nodules creating what appear to be spirit-like beings as if out of a fantasy land. As you contemplate and observe more closely you can even see what look like the faces of ancient elders.

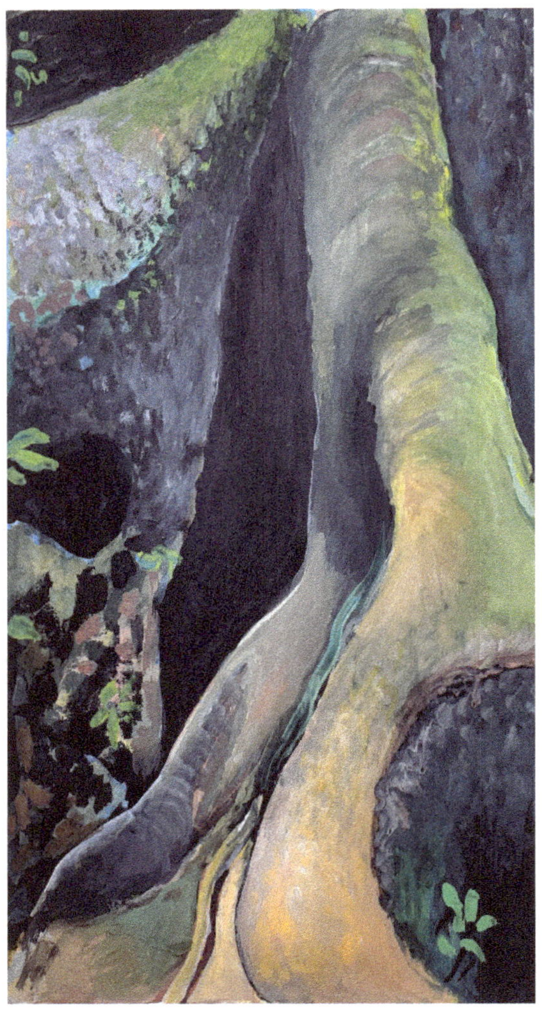

Antarctic Beech Tree, a Relic of Past Antiquity

Tree Plea

Eddie Dowd

I am in danger.
I have lived since time began
but now I am in danger
from you?
from myself?
incomplete creation is coming to a close
I am stifling
I need help
I am not beyond help.

Light flickers and fades
grows strong again
but not for me.
By myself
I am longing for life
I like to live
to breathe
to share my life
my shade
my wind
my being.

I am from all
I give to all
and you are taking it from me.
Uncaring eyes

Springbrook National Park encompasses 6,558 hectares and consists of four main sections—Springbrook plateau, Mount Cougal, Natural Bridge and the Numinbah Valley.

Natural Bridge, accessed from Numinbah Valley at the base of Springbrook, has been contoured by an ongoing process of erosion with rainfall feeding into streams and waterfalls. The power of swirling waters over millions of years has carved away volcanic rock and broken through into the cave below.

If you visit Natural Bridge at night you stand beneath a galaxy of luminance creatures. These are the tiny glow worms.

The area is truly remarkable for its ancient history and ecological significance. Springbrook is home to cascading waterfalls, dense rain forests, fresh mountain air, ancient trees, phenomenal vistas, and natural beauty.

Yugambeh people lived in the region for tens of thousands of years carefully implementing land management practices and using the country's rich natural resources.

Shaun Davies, a local Yugambeh man and language researcher, who was interviewed in the ABC documentary *Back To Nature*, says Springbrook is the intersection of different clan groups.

The Tweed people are over in the east, to the northeast and Gold Coast are the Kombumerri people, and over in the west beyond the ranges are the Mununjali and Migani.

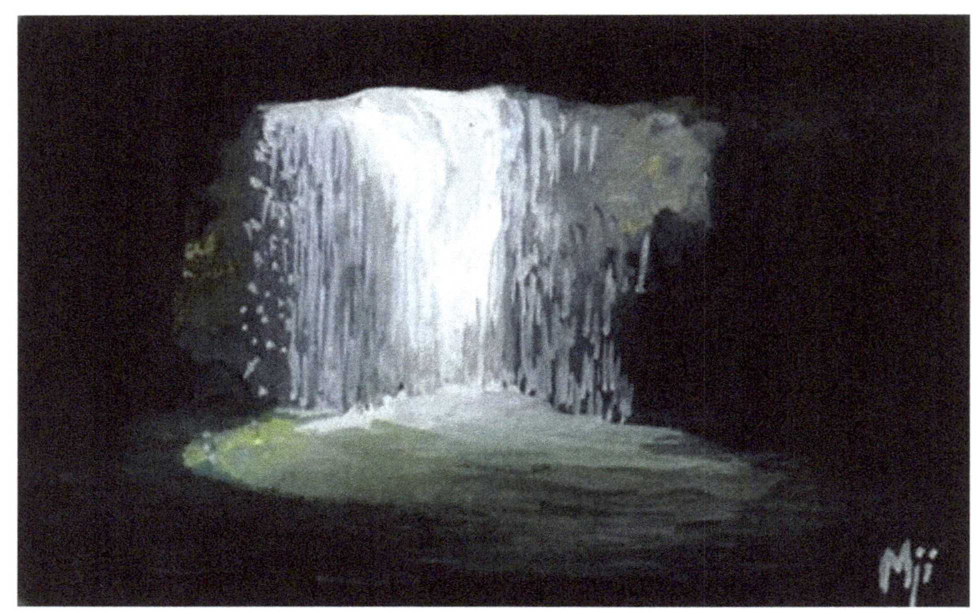

Natural Bridge, Numinbah Valley

Springbrook is Yugambeh Country and the Yugambah people are composed of nine clans –

Wangerriburra,
Bullongin,
Gugingin,
Migunberri,
Mununjali,
Tulginin,
Murangmuburra,
Cudgenburra, and,
Kombumerri.

The Yugambeh are the traditional custodians of the Country in southeast Queensland and northeast New South Wales, and also within the Logan City, Gold Coast, Scenic Rim, and Tweed City regions whose forebears all spoke one or more dialects of the Yugambeh Language.

Springbrook and its neighbouring mountains contain sacred places. These sites of special significance are spiritual places and are the spiritual home of Yugambeh clan groupings who shared language, ceremonies, celebrations and economic exchange.

As such this special Country has to be taken care of, nurtured and treated with respect and reverence.

There is power in telling the stories of this Country for there is an interconnected relationship between the earth, the water, rocks, plants, human, animals, creation ancestors, and the spirit world - all of life working together to support all of life.

Traditional stories tell of spirit creatures that reside in the mountains like the little hairy men who live in the bush at the bottom of the ranges.

Then there are also the other spirit beings, larger creatures, who live in the rainforest and if offended can cause misfortune like landslides.

While they live in the spirit world they can enter the human world where they can be cheeky and mischievous.

Chapter 6

Let's Paint

Are you ready now to visit Springbrook and be inspired by Country?

Be well prepared for a painting expedition.

First of all, I will give you some tips for painting outdoors.

Here you will learn how to choose your subject matter, to paint a compelling outdoor composition and, by using the subtleties of gouache water colour, to create beautifully expressive subjects and themes while exploring this exciting and expressive medium.

Tips

- plan ahead,

- choose the appropriate time of day,

- keep it simple,

- carry as little as possible,

- keep your art pack light in case you need to walk,

- set up in the shade if possible,

- avoid the heat and getting sunburnt,

- avoid the glare,

- carry a water bottle and a bit of food,

- carry insect spray,

- a small container of salt is useful in case of leeches,

- wear a hat,

- wear long pants,

- solid shoes,

- carry a small folding, canvas stool to sit on.

Benefits of painting outdoors

If *plein air* painting appeals to you this can take place anywhere outside your home. It can happen in the Australian bush, in your garden, the local park, at the beach, the outback, or a tropical rainforest. It doesn't matter where — just so long as it is outdoors.

With *plein air* painting opportunity presents itself to become physically immersed in the landscape. Being in nature permeates the body. It can influence the way you walk. You will discover that you walk more slowly, and you will breathe more slowly.

The painter experiences the landscape through their senses bringing the senses alive. Feel the breeze on the skin, respond to what you see, sense the ambience of the landscape.

Listen to the sounds of the land. A bird chirping in the tree, a fly buzzing around, the distant sound of an engine, the cleansing effect of a trickle of water flowing into a billabong, the movement of a lizard in the bushes. Or the touch of a leaf, the feeling of leaves brushing on your body as you walk past a bush.

Sense the magnetic energy of Country.

Not only at this sensory level but you respond intellectually, spiritually and historically to place. At Springbrook you travel back in time with the history of the area.

For millions of years this country has been formed, shaped and moulded to its present-day existence. It goes back to a past when dinosaurs roamed the land.

At the cultural level, it is Country that has been nurtured by people, cared for and managed. Yugembah custodians tended the land and developed a deep spiritual connection with it, telling its stories, respecting the country for it has been home to the precious elders for centuries.

Plein air painting is about going back to nature, going beyond one's comfort zone, increasing one's powers of observation, and absorbing the healing qualities of the environment you are in. It helps with the reduction of stress, calms the body, lowers the blood pressure, reduces anxiety, and aids relaxation and mental and physical recovery.

The artist can get out there in Country and have some fun and enjoyment. By using gouache paint going bush is easy because the gouache paint tubes are small and light; they are versatile, easy to transport and easy to clean up.

Gouache is brilliant for landscape painting. The painter can work fast, focus on the subtle and ever-changing qualities of light, simplify and become more confident with the brush, depict the true colours of a scene, and convey the essence and feeling of the place.

My *Plein Air* Painting Excursions

In my painting career I've always loved painting outdoors. I first started experimenting with gouache when my partner, Alex Barlow, and I travelled to the south of France. We stayed in Van Gogh country and spent a few days in Arles.

I remember our walking out into the countryside and climbing a hill where we could survey the French countryside with our picnic of a baguette and goat's cheese. I carried with me my new gouache paints, a couple of brushes, a water colour pad of paper, and a small container of water. It was here that I painted for the first time with my gouache paints.

Apart from my love of gouache I really appreciated the fact that the tubes of paint were very small and light, making carrying one's art gear easily transportable —. that makes them easy to carry on an aeroplane, travelling by car, or in a backpack while hiking.

Since that time in the south of France painting with gouache has become my primary method for making paintings.

Making pictures with gouache is so conducive to *plein air* painting. Grab a portable chair, put your gouache paints, brushes and small water colour pad into your backpack, and head off to your favourite place by the ocean or in the countryside. Spend the day making paintings!

One of my memorable painting trips was to the Charters Towers goldfields. Alex and I remember staying in an old Queenslander backpackers' accommodation in Charters Towers.

It was January and we were experiencing really terrible, excessive heat. The road outside was so hot you could have fried an egg on the bitumen.

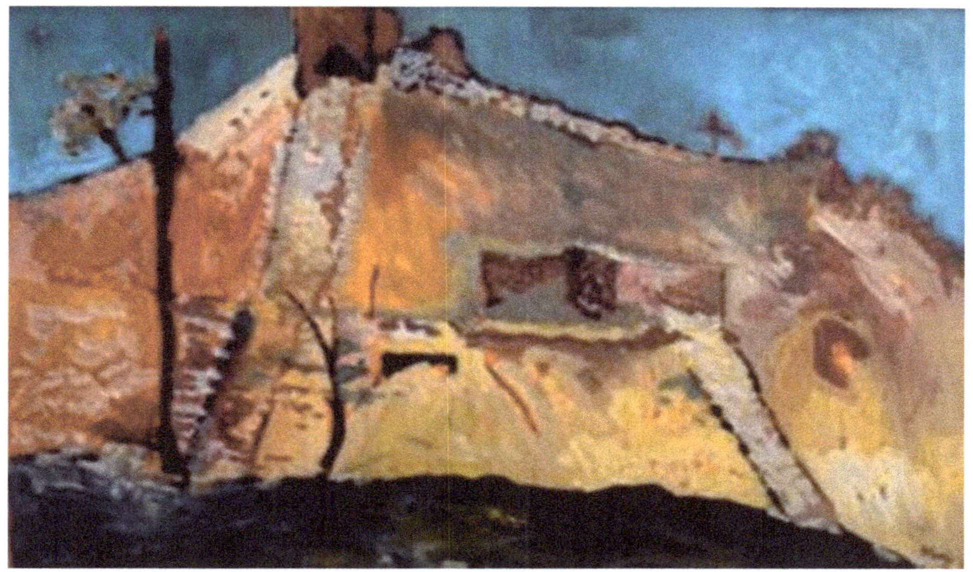

Old Workings on the Charter's Towers Gold Field

Trying to paint during the day was impossible. My plan was to make a series of landscapes of the old, Charters Towers goldfields.

I had to plan my *plein air* painting excursions for just after sunrise. At sunrise we would leave the backpackers and go on to the gold fields where I'd set up to paint.

Because of the extreme heat, the painting experience was uncomfortable. I had to paint fast so that I could return to the backpackers to escape the heat.

Over the two weeks that we were in Charters Towers I made a series of about ten small, gouache paintings. By 7am, when the day really started to heat up, we would return to our base with my latest painting for the day.

By the time we had to leave Charters Towers I had created a good body of work and I had a successful exhibition of these paintings in a Canberra gallery.

My painting career has been dotted by excursions into Country. In contrast to Queensland, I made a fabulous trip to Charlottes Pass in the Australian Alps.

We stayed for a few days at Charlottes Pass at the grand old lady of the mountains, the Kosciuszko Chalet. It was summertime and we explored the idyllic spring and summer alpine scenery with its wildflowers, snow gums and glacial lakes.

The Alps have always been inspirational for *plein air* painting. I would set up among the wildflowers and alpine heath and make paintings on canvas using acrylic paints.

I became a bit of an attraction for the tourists who would love to come over, inspect my painting and have a chat.

I'm not sure if this was a benefit or one of the challenges of *plein air* painting.

On the Gold Coast, regular visits to Couran Cove on South Stradbroke Island was another inspirational place for painting.

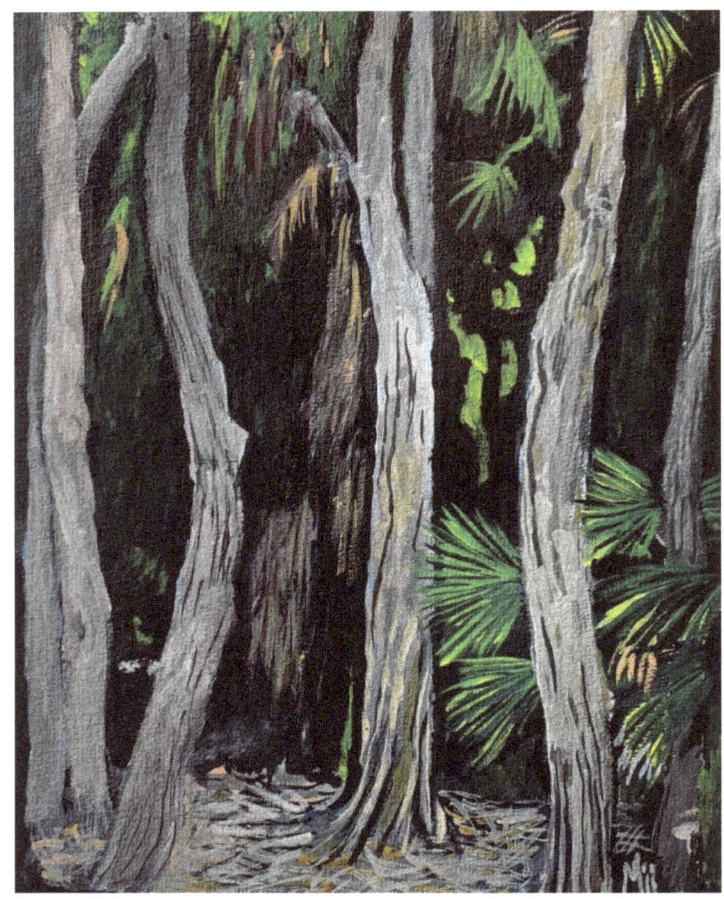

Rainforest at Couran Cove, South Stradbroke Island, Qld

Other memorable *plein air* painting trips were to Lake Eucumbene at the base of the alpine area, Wallaga Lake on south coast of New South Wales, and art excursions with fellow art students from what was then the Canberra School of Art. We painted at Jervis Bay.

We also made another art trip to Eden on the coast near the border between Victoria and New South Wales.

I lived for a few years at Mosman Bay in Sydney. This was an artist's mecca with the harbour, its boats, luxuriant and lush foliage, bird and wildlife all in the heart of Sydney.

Tom Roberts and Arthur Streeton came to Sydney in the 1890s and they were among those captivated by Sydney Harbour. They spent considerable time painting around the harbour.

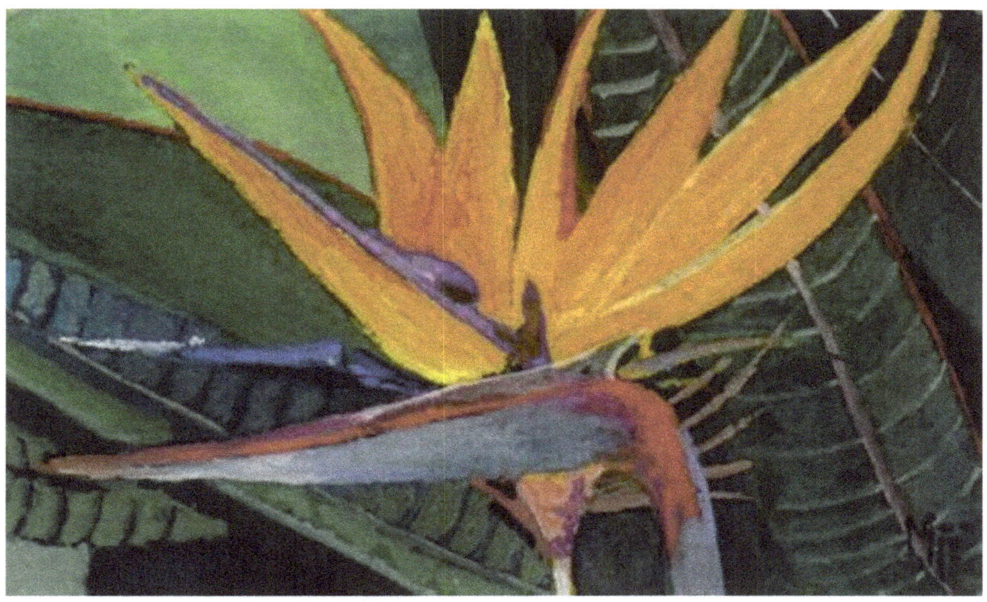

Bird of Paradise at Mosman Bay, Sydney

Personally, I found it a great source of inspiration so I could really understand why it was so popular for the early painters. Here I made a lot of paintings — small works on paper — and started also to explore the art of card making as a result of my art experience in the local Mosman Bay environment.

Mosman was the inspiration for many *plein air* painters of early Sydney. In the 1880s and 1890s artists' camps flourished around Sydney Harbour particularly in the Mosman area.

Getting Ready

When planning to paint outdoors or go on a painting expedition, you need to get well organised in advance. If you miss something like forgetting to bring a small folding seat to sit on or some water and a jar to dip your brushes in could play havoc with your excursion.

Just think, you travel all the way to the place where you want to paint. If you don't want to stand up at an easel and you want to sit down while you paint and if there are no large rocks around you will have a problem if you have nothing to sit on. How your painting excursion could be totally wrecked!

I cannot stress enough to get well organised in advance with a checklist of what you need to take with you.

Checklist for a *plein air* painting expedition

- gouache paints,

- mixing tray - palette or even just a paper palette,

- brushes - about 3 small brushes of different sizes,

- block of water colour paper,

- water for drinking,

- water for painting,

- small water jar,

- easel – optional,

- folding canvas seat,

- folding table – optional,

- insect spray,

- salt (leeches are common in a damp, rainforest environment),

- hat,

- sunscreen,

- protective clothing - boots, thick socks, trousers,

- food or snacks,

- rags,

- backpack,

- iPhone for taking photographs.

Overcoming the challenges

Plein air painting is not without its challenges.

First and foremost is having to carry the artist's equipment to the site. Then you have to set everything up.

The French box easel, a significant invention of art equipment for artists on the 19th century, is easy to fold up into the size of a briefcase. This makes it easy to transport and easy to store.

Another development in painting equipment is the Pochade Box. This compact box has space for painters to store their painting supplies.

I recommend keeping things simple. Don't take too much on a *plein air* art expedition. While you will need some paints, paper, brushes and water you don't really need to take an easel or proper palette.

Be prepared to improvise. The water and pallet can be put on the ground, sit on a small folding, canvas stool, and make sure everything fits into a backpack.

The problem of carrying wet canvases home can be resolved by painting with water-based paint like gouache. If you choose to paint with oils the challenges would be greater.

Oils on canvas take a long time to dry and it's all just too easy for the canvas to get messed up.

But painting with gouache is easy and it's easy to clean. It dries fast so there is not the same risk that you have with oil paint.

With *plein air* painting, focus on using water-based paint like gouache. It's so transportable, it is quick drying, and carrying a block of water colour paper is easier than transporting a canvas.

Navigating the weather is perhaps the greatest challenge for *plein air* painters. Weather conditions and exposure to the elements such as coping with the heat, wind, or rain is a challenge.

Then there are the insects - ants, flies, and various bugs like little caterpillars that can fall out of a tree or off a shrub. You can be comfortably set up and then find you are attracting certain types of insects.

I remember how off-putting it was when I was sitting beneath a poinciana tree only to discover that soon I was the target for caterpillars dropping out of the tree.

Then one of the less appealing features of painting in the rainforest are the leeches. Leeches are my pet peeve. If the rainforest is very damp you can find a leech has attached itself to your body sucking your blood.

Leeches love wet and moist environments so don't be surprised if you find small leeches finding their way onto your body. For this reason, always carry a salt cellar so that you can get rid of a leech by covering it in salt.

I can remember when I was about eight years old having an afternoon swim in the Barwon River at Mungindi near the New South Wales/Queensland border. I was horrified at finding a huge leech attached to my bottom.

You will find leeches in almost every patch of a moist rainforest and even on dry riverbanks.

Like forests everywhere, ticks are another hazard. The scrub tick is a danger for *plein air* painters. If you are bitten by tick, remove it, and if it is a scrub tick, consult a doctor. Early symptoms of tick paralysis include headache and nausea.

And last and not least watch out for snakes. Snakes are common in the rainforest. They are mostly secretive, or they can be found high in the trees. Many species are highly venomous. Make sure you don't step on one or bother it. Watch where you walk and give a wide berth to any you encounter.

A Painting Excursion to Springbrook

The date was set for a painting excursion to Springbrook. The planning was complete and the backpack filled with painting supplies. My friends, Mary and Sherien, were coming with me and Sherien had prepared the picnic lunch.

But the day dawned damp with spots of rain on the window.

Oh no!

What was the weather going to do? I had real feelings of apprehension as I looked out at the horizon over the ocean.

A weak sunrise was attempting to lighten the day. The sky was heavy with cloud! There were occasional showers.

Out over the ocean were patches of sun and then patches of rain cloud. Not a good look for the day's painting trip.

Was this painting excursion even going to happen? If it was wet here on the coast, the mountains would probably be even worse!

Despite my feelings of apprehension, I proceeded with my plans and headed for the mountains.

We drove into the hinterland and stopped at the Hinze Dam for a coffee. Surprisingly, the area was dry. This was a good omen. If it was dry at the dam, there was every chance it would be dry at Springbrook.

So, with my friends in tow, I drove up the winding road to Springbrook. It was dry but there was a bit of moisture in the air. Clouds hung low, however, at the end of the road.

We decided that Purling Brook picnic ground would be the best place for painting. There was plenty of shelter there just in case there was rain.

I surveyed the surrounding rainforest looking for suitable subject matter. I identified a couple of spots that looked worthwhile with the companionship of an inquisitive brush turkey, a friendly kookaburra, a seasonally cranky magpie, and a crow lookalike, the currawong.

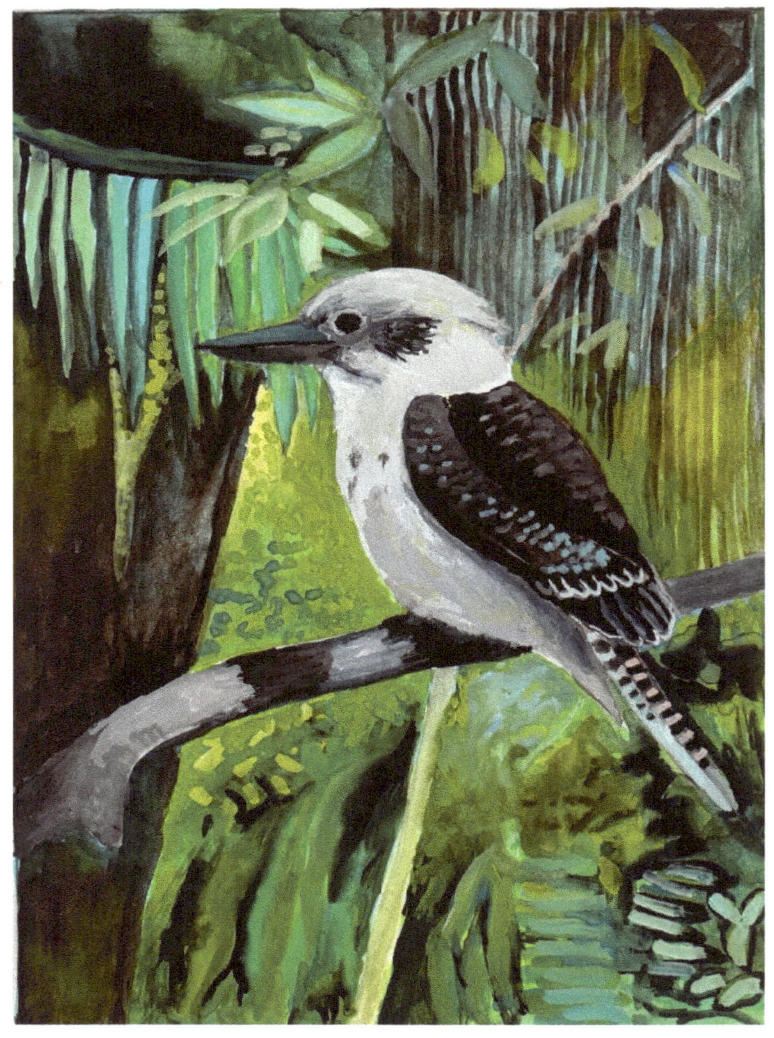

Springbrook Kookaburra

Happily, I'm relieved to say that on this excursion there were no leeches, no ticks, no snakes, and no creepy crawlies.

I even found a suitable rock to sit on. My plan was to make a couple of quick sketches with my gouache paints.

The focus of my first sketch were some a large dark tree trunks against the rich green rainforest. I was happily painting away when low and behold - a family of picnickers arrived and set up at the picnic table at the base of the tree.

Drat!

I kept my cool. I couldn't exactly tell them they couldn't park themselves there.

As I was still able to get a fairly clear vision of the trunk of my tree, I proceeded with what I was doing. It was just a bit distracting having this family parked there almost blocking the view of my subject matter. Again, one of the challenges of painting *plein air*.

Chapter 7

Painting with Gouache

Other names for gouache paint are gouache water colour or opaque water colour. Gouache is not dissimilar to water colour paint because you mix it with water and the brushes are cleaned with water.

As you paint gouache can be diluted with water to make the paint more transparent. But I think its charm is in building up blocks of colour which can be made to be rich and vibrant. If you keep building up colour over colour you can generate a magnificent intensity.

Gouache is not something new; it has been around for centuries. There was gouache-like paint in Greek and Egyptian times, temperas which used egg yolk as a binder.

Painting with gouache became popular in the 1800s when the French Impressionists started going out into the countryside, painting in the open air.

The Impressionists liked gouache because it was easy to use and convenient to use when painting outdoors. You could use it to paint quickly.

Gouache paints dried quickly. Oil paints, on the other hand, were complicated and messy to use outdoors and they took such a long time to dry.

Gouache might be a close relative of water colour paint but it is still a very different medium.

It varies in consistency. This depends on how much water you add. Gouache can range from being very watery to a consistency that is quite thick, a bit like what you can achieve with acrylics or oil paint.

The same gum Arabic binder that is used in water colour is also used in gouache — a thick, glutinous water-soluble medium —but it has more pigment which is not ground as finely as in water colour.

Where watercolours are transparent, gouache mixes coloured pigments with an opaque white pigment, often chalk. The chalk (calcium carbonate) is an addition to the paint and makes the gouache look flat and opaque.

Gouache is quite different to transparent water colour painting which is executed on brilliant, white, high quality water colour paper. With gouache you can create great sweeps of smooth and immaculate slabs of colour.

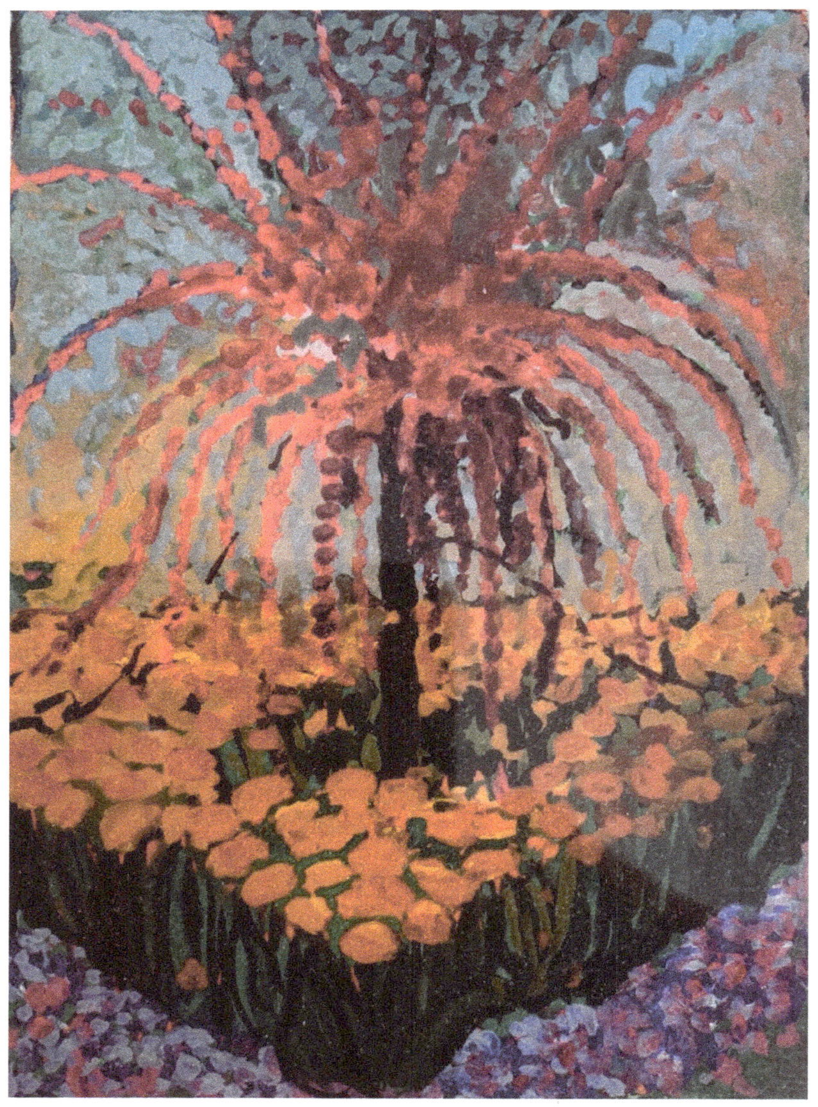

Tulip Farm outside Canberra

Drying so quickly, gouache paint can be easily reworked. This is an exciting feature because, even when the painting has been finished, it can be reworked by painting over previous work.

In contrast to acrylic paint which is thicker, more durable, and waterproof, gouache is fragile. It does not have the same durability as acrylic.

An accidental droplet of water or watery gouache onto the painting can result in a watery blob and totally mess up the picture.

When it dries gouache looks heavy, dense, and opaque but when water is added, gouache becomes more translucent. You have the option of either watering the paint down or you can build it up the consistency of the paint.

The end result can be a painting which is radiant and bright but which has a matte finish. Gouache is excellent for small or medium sized works. I use it for making my art cards which are really miniature paintings and I also use it for painting medium sized art pieces.

For large paintings I use acrylics. It is tough, it's waterproof, and it has the durability. I used oils in past years.

While acrylic paint can be used on paper, glass, canvas, plastic, and wood it is best to use gouache on water colour paper although some artists do use it on canvas.

Gouache is a great medium to use particularly if you want to experiment. You can build up areas of your painting and can then paint over the top of previously applied gouache.

It's easy to make changes as I've already said. If something is not working for you just paint over that patch. For instance, if you are completely shattered by the bit you have just created, paint it out and redo it.

You keep painting until you get the result you want.

Gouache is versatile; it has fantastic colours, and these colours can be watered down or they can be built up or layered.

Painting techniques

Experiment with gouache and you will discover for yourself what you can and cannot do with gouache.

Many newcomers to this mode of artwork are a little cautious, thinking there is a "correct way" to paint.

Nothing could be further from the truth.

This is a delightful medium, one that grows with your confidence and ability. It's almost as if it is inviting you to have fun, to experiment, to go beyond your own expectation.

There is nothing comparable to discovering the talent hidden within you, gouache-wise.

That said, here are some of the ways open for you to explore:

- Staining
- Glazing
- Dry Brushing
- Opaque layering
- Blooms
- Splatters
- Reworking
- Colour Blending

Staining: One technique is staining and this involves covering an area of the paper with a thin consistency of watered-down gouache. This can be a foundation from where you will grow your painting.

Glazing: As you thin down gouache with water, you can then you layer it on top of areas that have already been painted and which are dry. This is called glazing and this enriches the colour or it can create a new colour.

Dry brushing: Another technique is dry brushing. You put paint onto your brush and then eliminate most of that paint. Apply the brush quickly to the paper with no water. As you brush across the paper different effects and textures can be created.

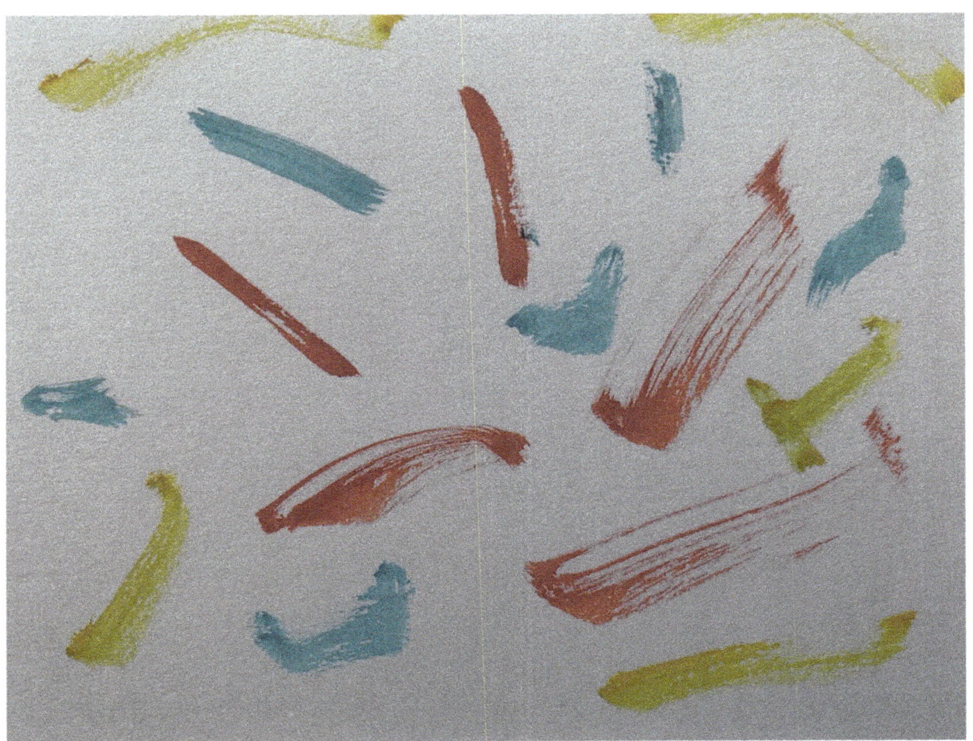

Opaque layering: Creating additional layers of gouache without using much water is called opaque layering. By doing this you can achieve a rich colour which is opaque.

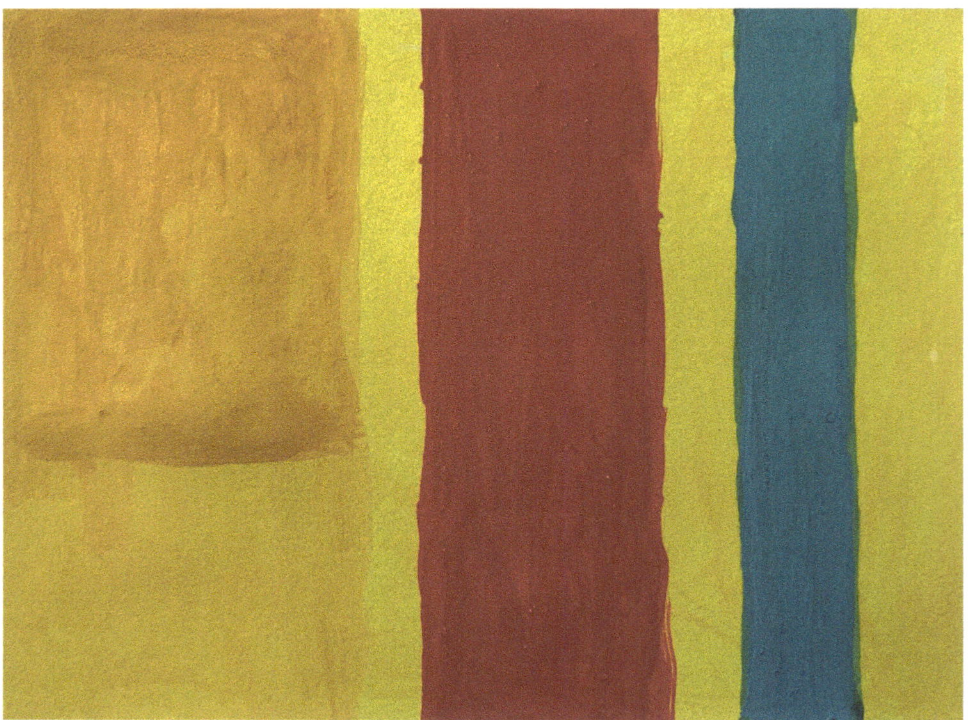

This opaque colour can completely cover anything that was underneath so mistakes or anything else can easily be removed.

Beware…

I warn you that gouache can crack if you add too many layers of thick paint to the same spot.

Blooms: Irregular patches of colour can be made when you add lots of water and just a little bit of paint to the brush. These are blooms. This blob of colour can then bleed and spread across the paper creating interesting effects.

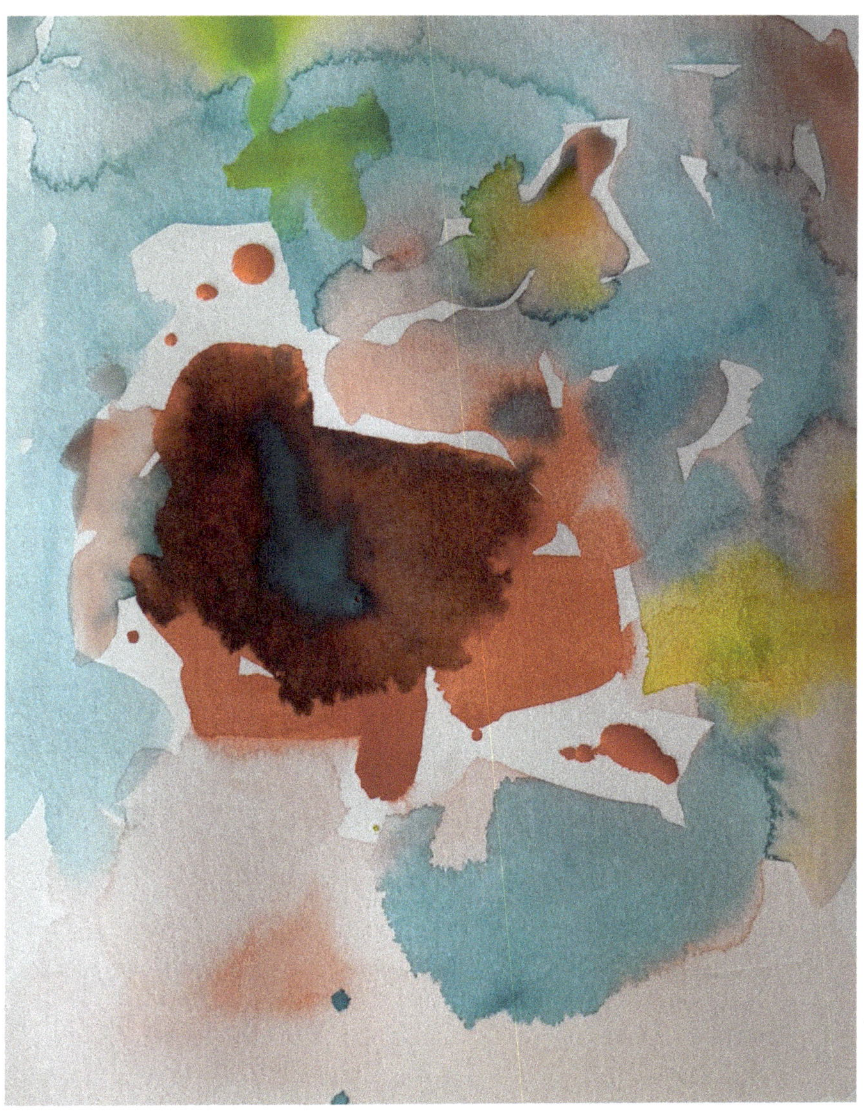

Splatters: Then there are splatters. This is when you flick the paint onto the paper again creating special effects.

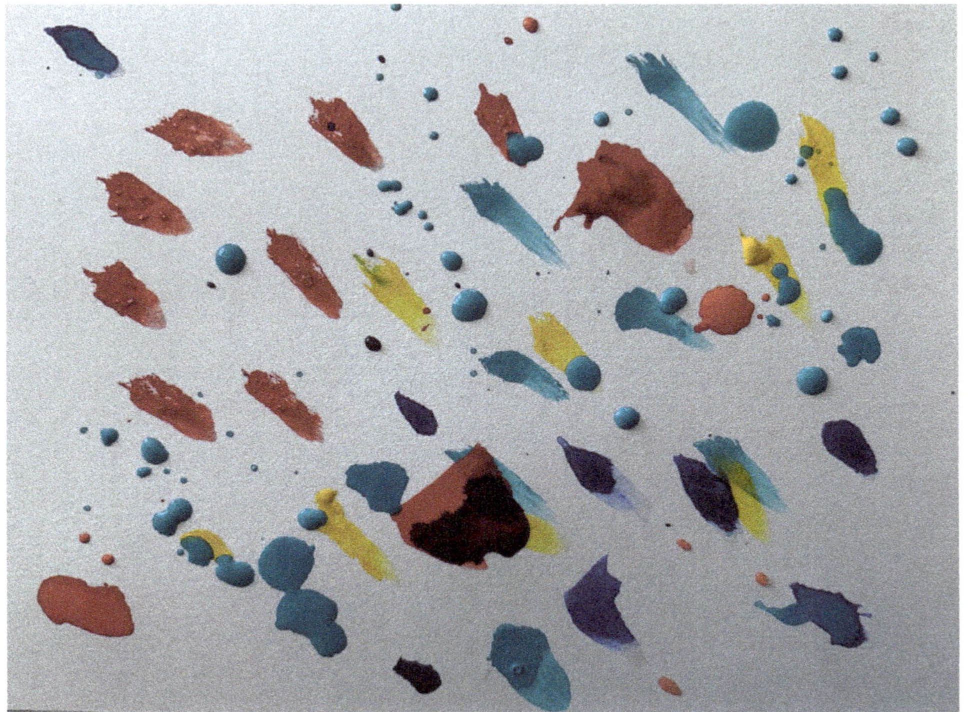

Reworking: Once a gouache painting has dried, it is possible to wet it again. This way, you can create a different and interesting look by reworking and re-painting different areas.

Sometimes the muse compels you to add or subtract a feature that differs from your original creation.

No problems. Reworking is just what you need.

Colour blending: The technique of colour blending involves blending colours actually on the paper. An interesting result can be produced by putting a colour onto the paper and then adding another colour until they mix.

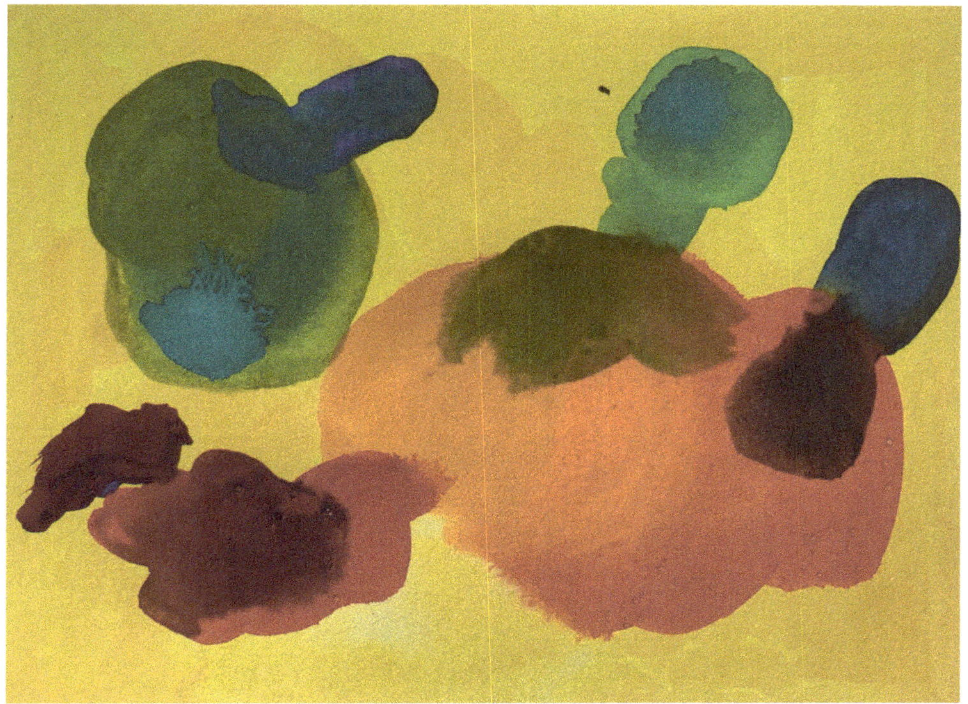

If you paint wet gouache onto wet or damp paper, you can end up with blurred effects and soft shapes.

Protecting your gouache painting

A gouache painting does need to be protected.

You have already learnt that if water is applied to a dry gouache painting it can reactivate the paint. A drop of water on your artwork can do the same thing except that it will wreck everything you have done — so beware of that errant droplet of water.

Put your painting under glass as soon as you can to protect it. This is what I do or you could visit the art shop, purchase a water colour vanish and seal the painting but this may not be without hazard as a heavy hand and excess varnish can act like adding water to the top layer of your finished product.

Chapter 8

How to Paint Outdoors

Make a painting

The Best of All Lookout in the Springbrook National Park is a very special site for painting. Not only is it where you find the ancient Antarctic beech trees with their gnarled and twisted roots as old as Christian religion it's a fantastic place from where you can enjoy the panoramic views of the region.

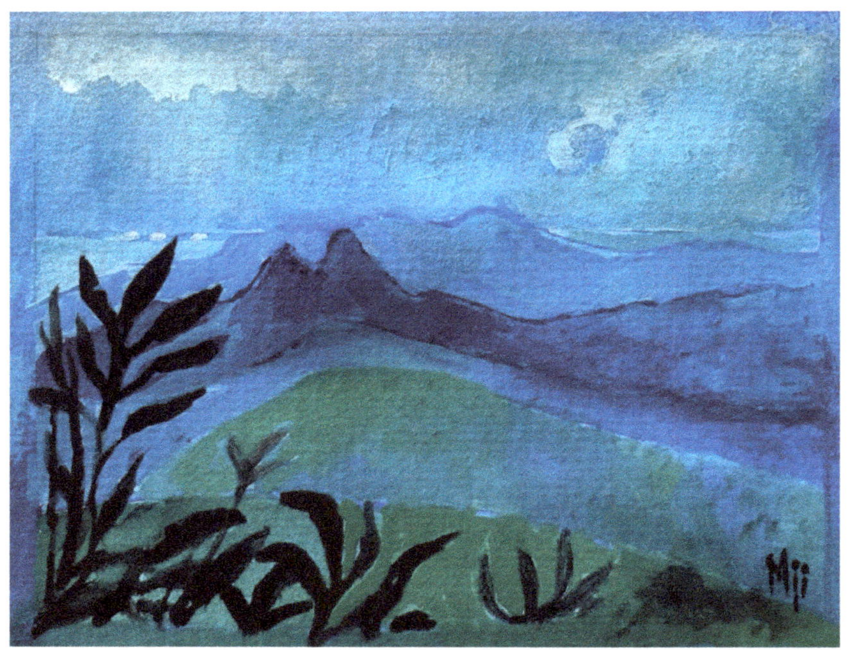

Best of All Lookout

At the lookout the views are amazing. You can look out over the entire plateau across the Queensland-New South Wales border towards Wollumbin and Byron Bay and see the remnants of ancient volcanic activity.

Get ready now to start painting.

Step 1

Decide on the size you want for your painting. My rule of thumb is to get the measurements from various stock frames, select a matching block of water colour paper, and then measure a size for your painting-to-be that will suit the stock frame.

The advantage of doing this is that as soon as you've completed your work, and you are happy with it, you can pop it into its frame.

This is a quick, inexpensive, and easy way to protect your painting.

If down the track you want to put it into a more up-market frame, you can easily do so and the stock frame is now available for reuse.

How convenient is that, eh?

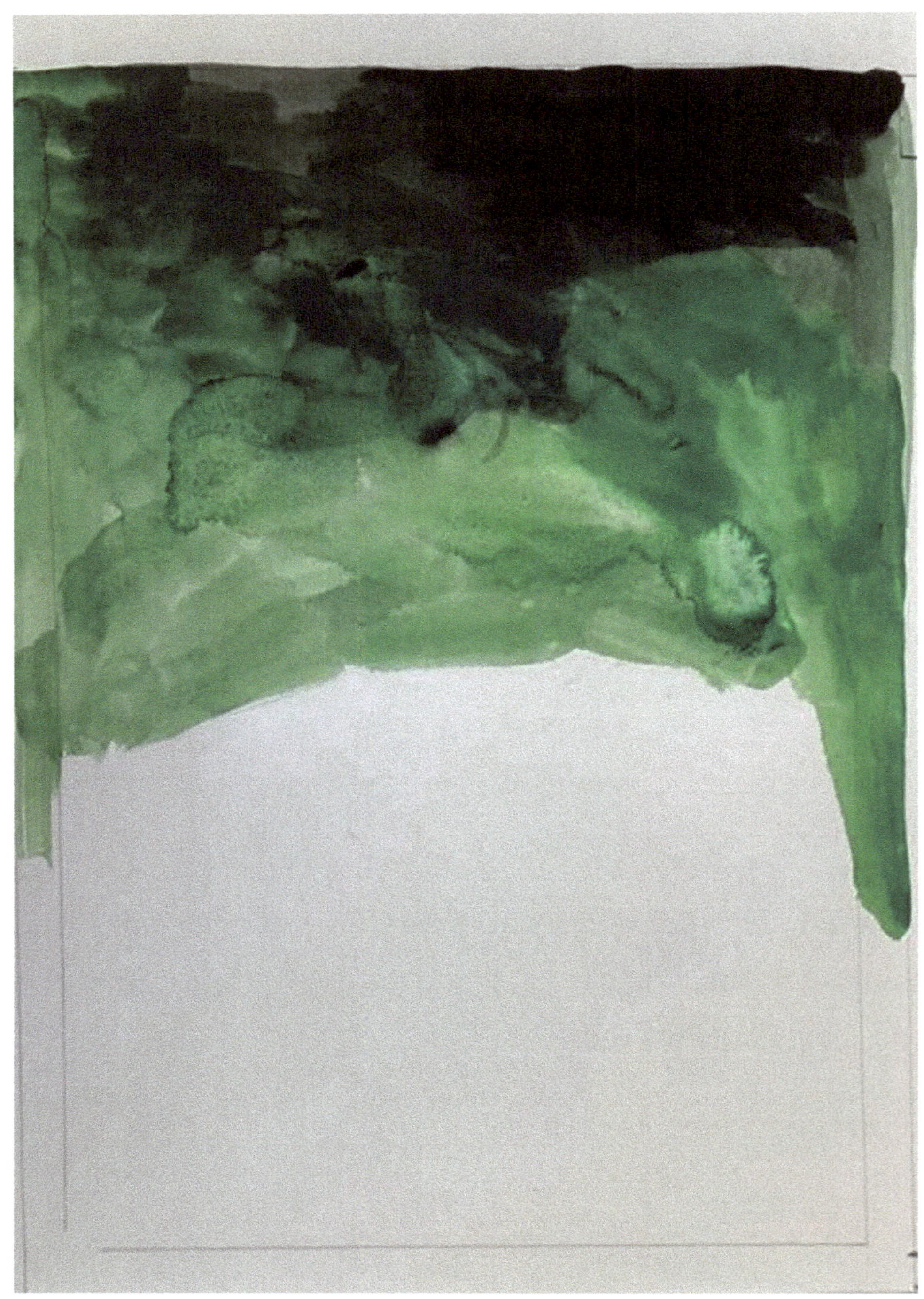

Step 2

When you have outlined the size, paint the entire area with a thin consistency of watered-down gouache. Remember, this is called staining.

This is the foundation from where you will build your painting. Use plenty of water, roughly apply the paint and don't worry about making it even.

Select a colour. I usually choose one that's going to blend with the other hues I will eventually use to make the painting.

You will find that gouache is user friendly. It's a popular medium for painting landscapes because of its transportability and versatility.

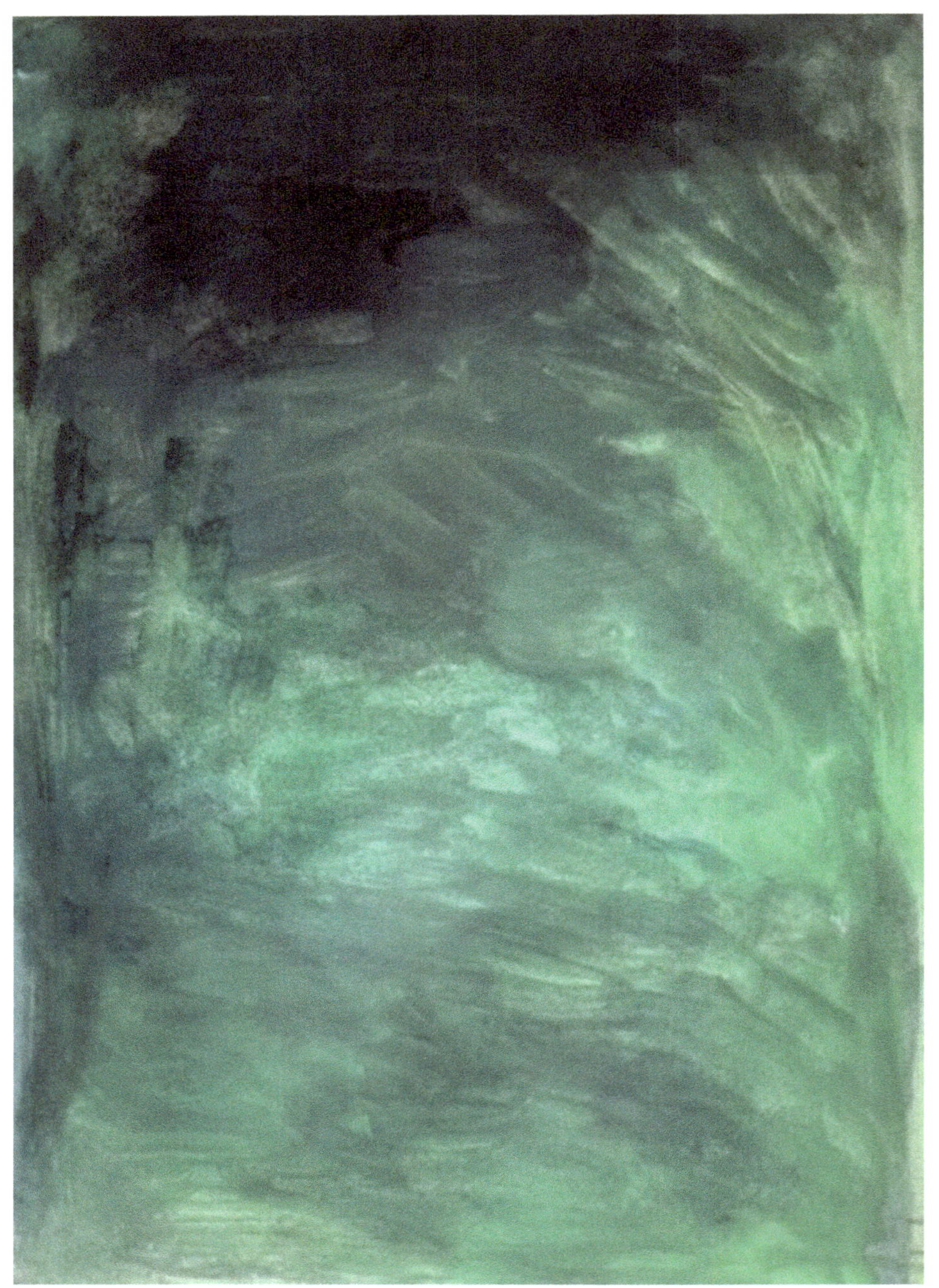

Step 3

A useful method is to make a thumbnail sketch prior to mapping out the composition. This will help you to abstract the general placement of the shapes for your composition.

Look at the shapes in front of you and simplify these into broad masses.

Avoid painting in any detail.

Don't add a leaf or a blade of grass. Instead, create a mass unifying the area with broad brush strokes. Detail can be added later if need be.

Then once you have the feel of the composition draft it out in paint straight on to the water colour block of paper.

All you are doing at this stage is roughly drawing an outline of the composition.

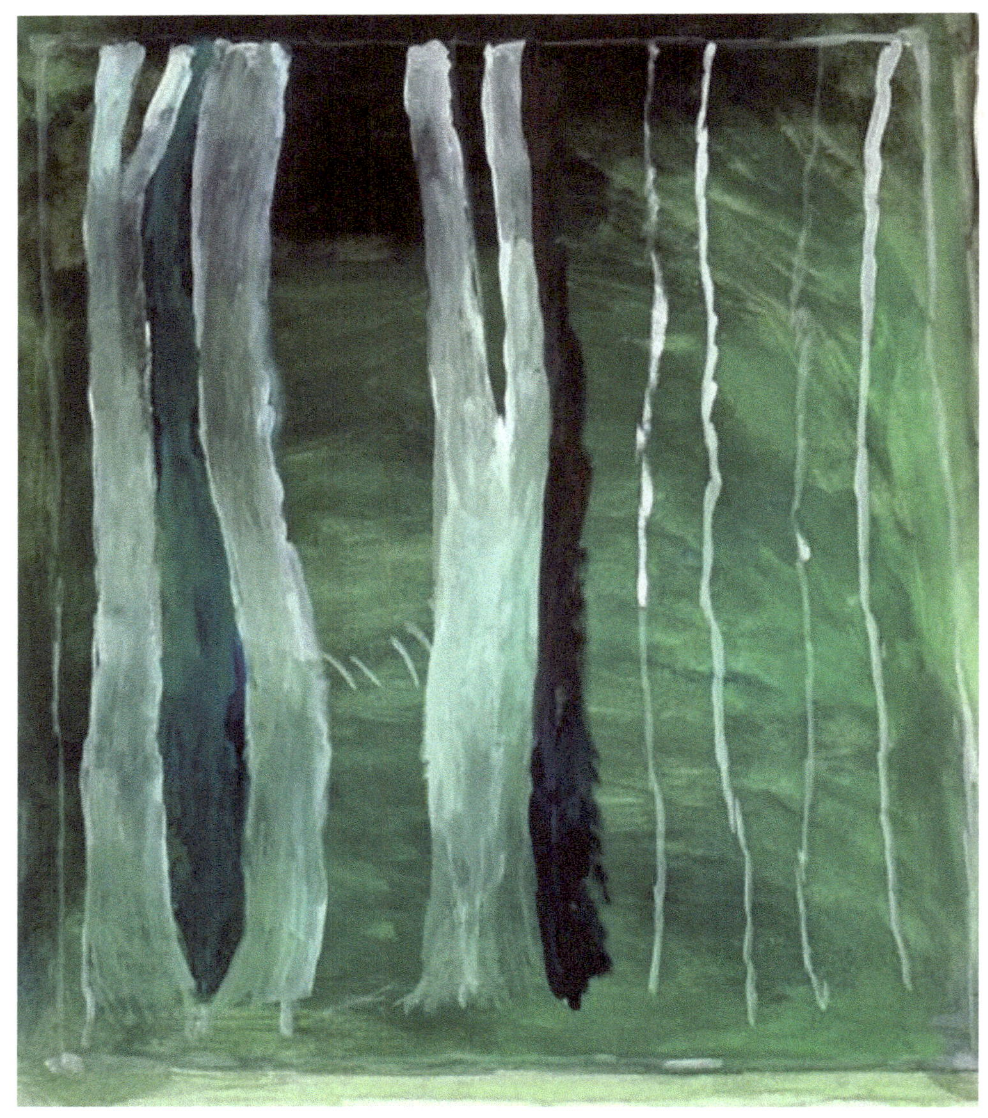

Page 92

Step 4

Next you can block in the composition with slabs of colour. Create a rough painting. Quickly work the painting as a whole and avoid concentrating on any detail.

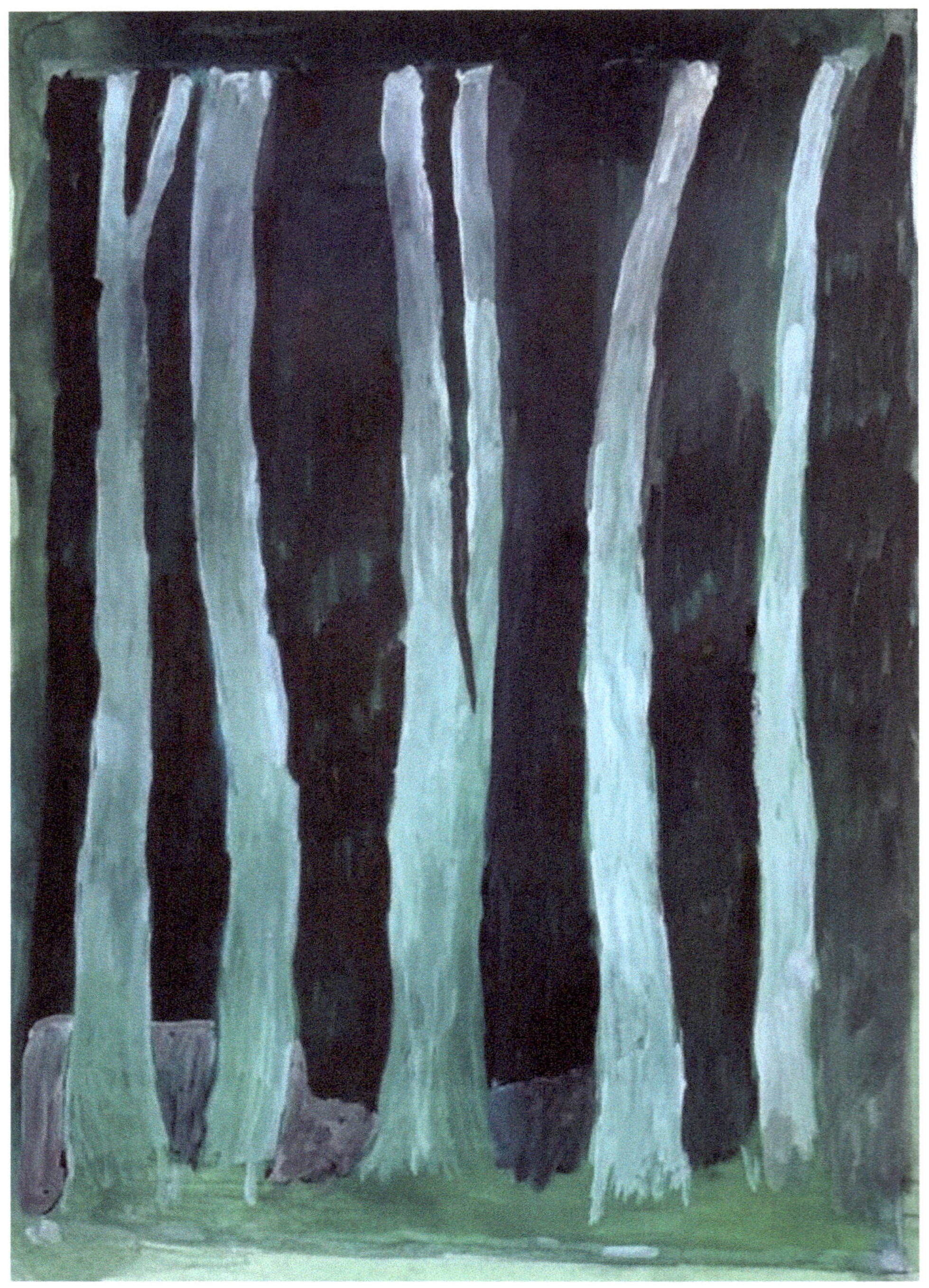

Step 5

In Step 5 you are taking the painting through to its final phrase. Start working now on the detail but be mindful of the painting as a whole.

Remember, I had you measure up the painting? Well, it's a good idea to extend the paint beyond the measured area.

Do this because when you go to put it in a frame you don't want to have any white area around the painting showing through accidentally, just in case your measurements are not quite accurate.

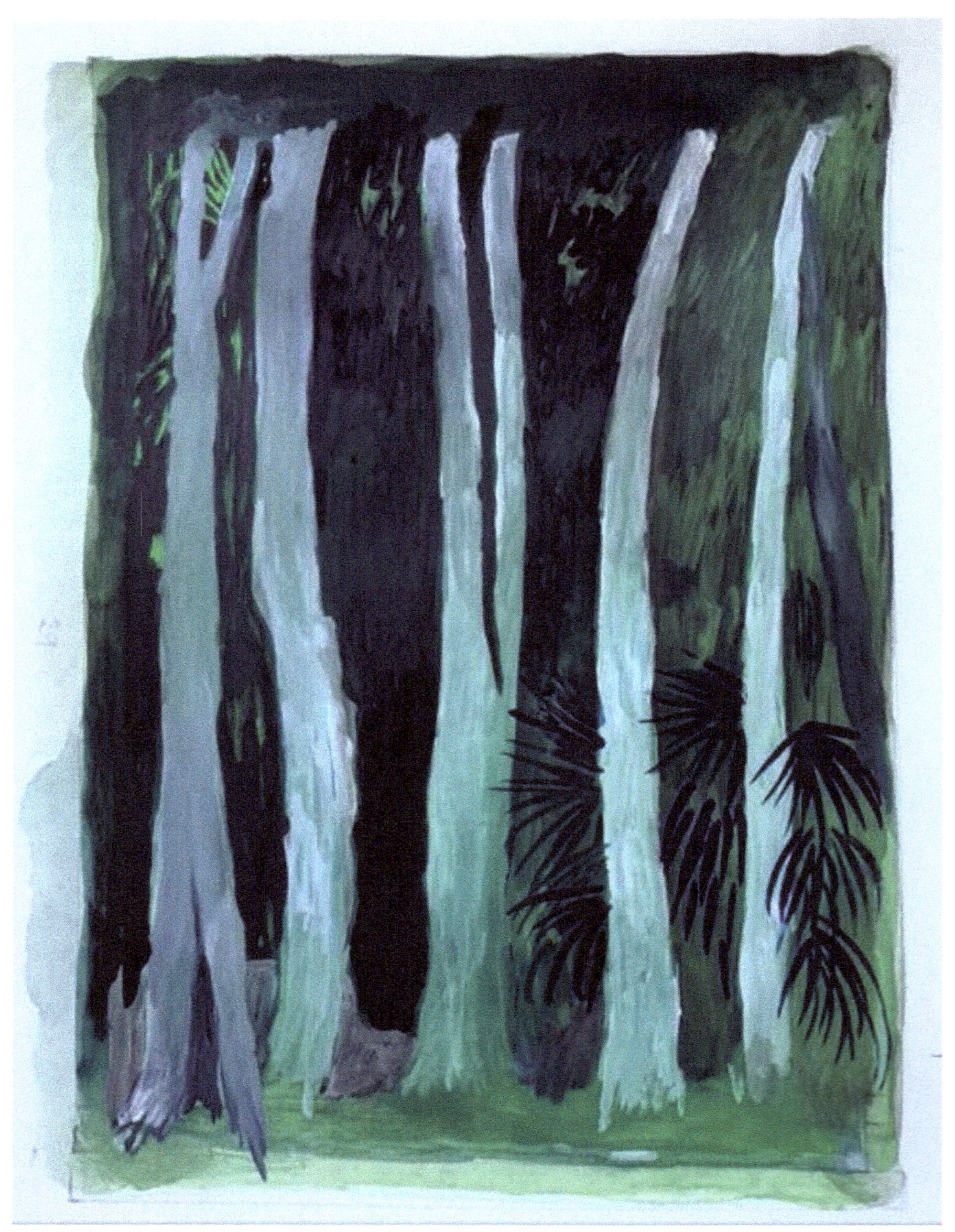

Step 6

As you paint the final phase of the painting keep building up the colour. Do this by create additional layers of gouache without using much water.

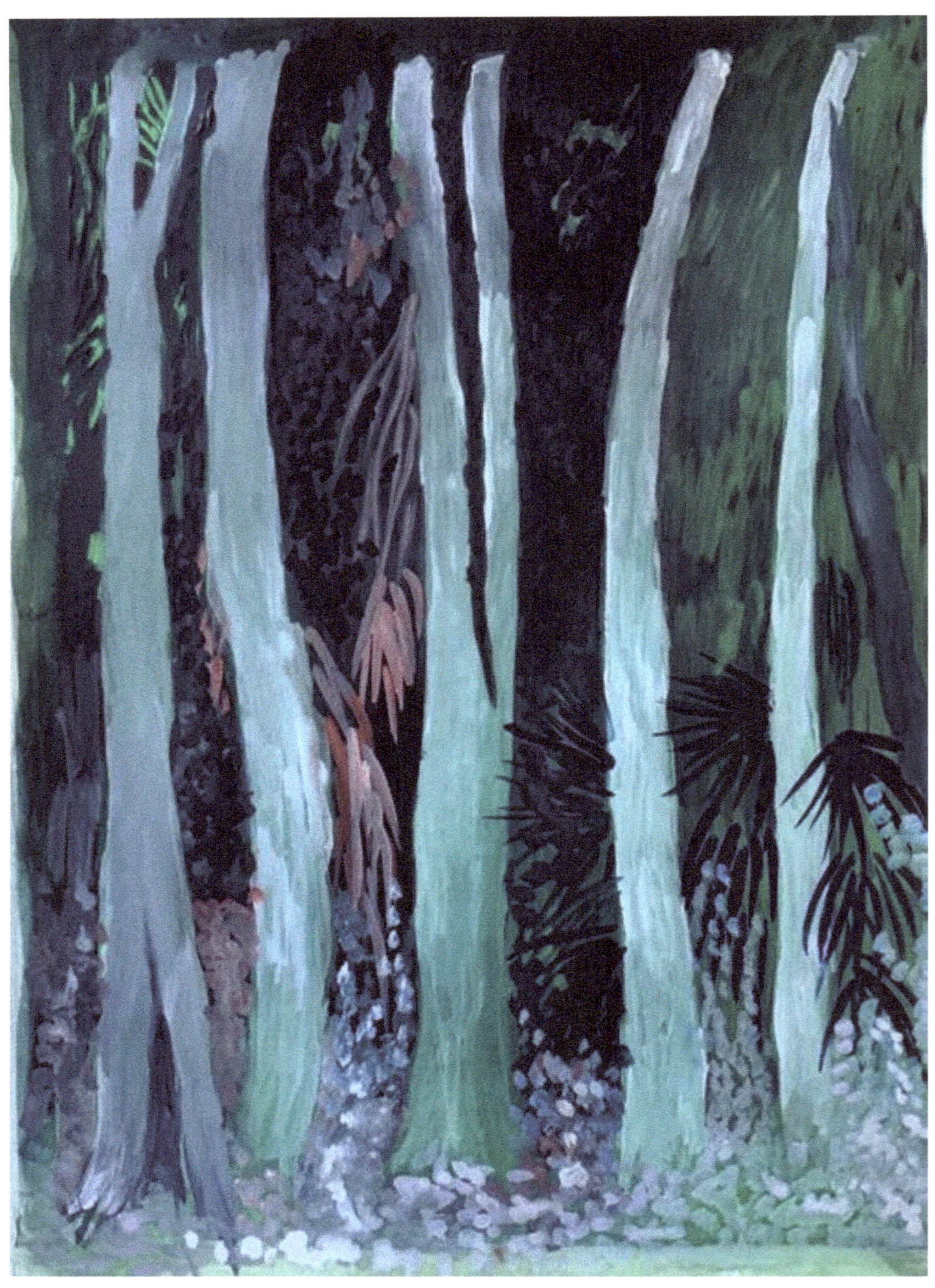

Step 7

If you don't like what you have done or have made a mistake this layering method allows you to cover up what you've already painted. Simply paint over anything you want removed.

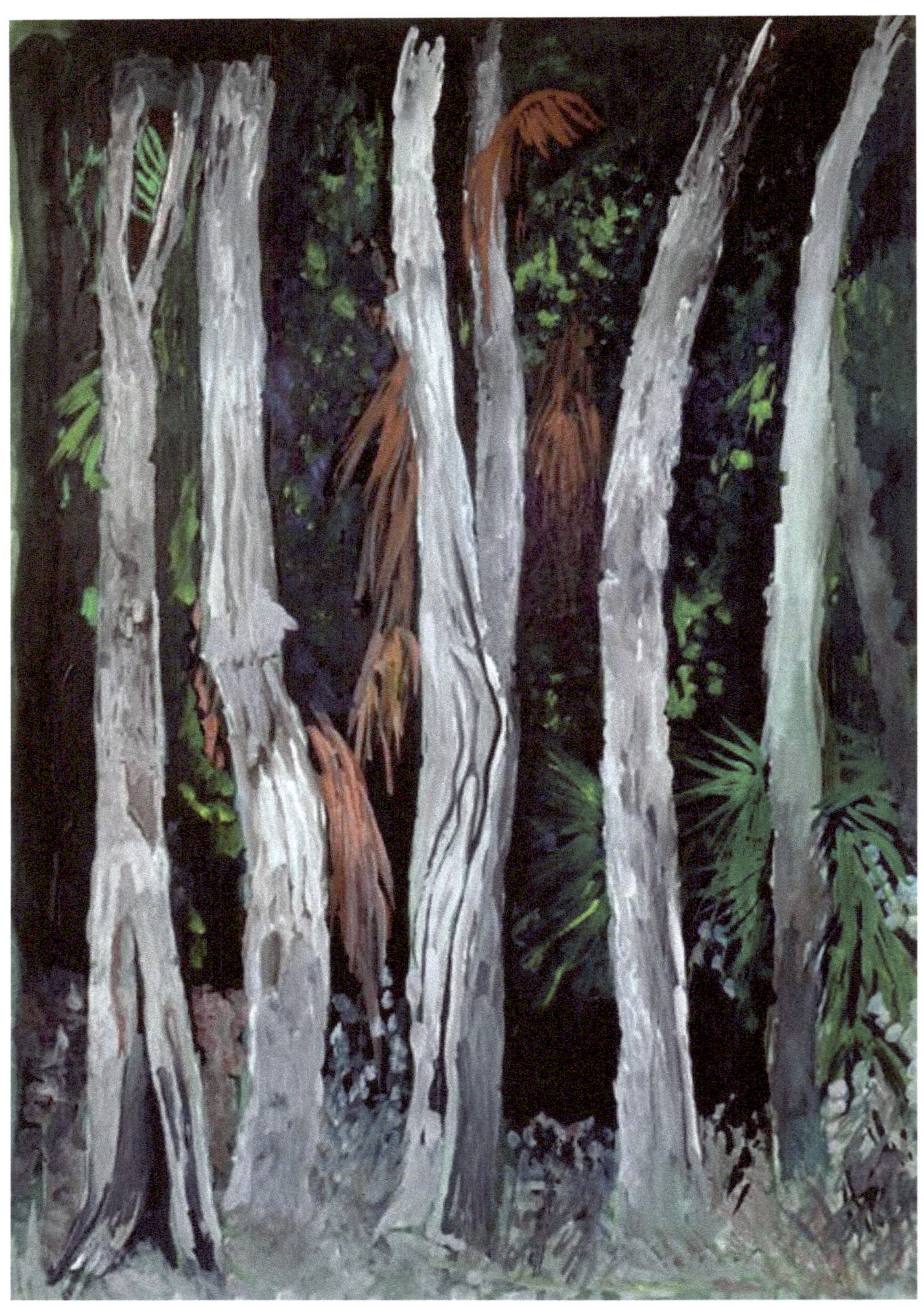

Choosing your subject matter

At Springbrook there is so much you can paint. You can paint the open vistas, you can focus on the landscape as it is in front of you, or you could paint a closeup, the detail of a fern or leaves, or a piece of bark.

When you choose your subject matter, don't try to incorporate everything you see in front of you otherwise you'll be overwhelmed.

Simplify the subject matter.

Make a few thumbnail sketches. This will help you choose what to focus on.

And don't overthink it.

Simply take quick action. Paint fast and don't worry about whether you'll make a successful painting or create a piece that will need a radical makeover.

It's a study and an exercise in observing the light, the atmosphere and subtleties of colour.

Plein air painting can fulfil different things:

- you can complete finished paintings in themselves that you can exhibit

- *Plein air* paintings can be works in progress. They can serve as a reference point for larger paintings that can be created back in the studio

- you can go into the landscape and take photographs and then use these images as starting points and ideas for landscape paintings.

- *Plein air* sketches can be used for colour referencing and as inspiration for studio paintings.

Using Photographs

While a useful aid, the idea is not to be married to a photograph nor do you attempt to replicate it. The photo is simply a starting point, a springboard, and a point of reference.

By combining *plein air* painting with photography you can use them both to good effect when creating larger studio works.

In Summary...

Plein air painting, even if not an end in itself, can be used for the research and development phase of your art and can be the fuel for creating exciting art pieces.

Painting Country and getting inspiration from a place like the Springbrook National Park is a journey back to nature and in the process takes you into another world. At one level it is a rewarding, artistic experience which can be full of joy, a healing, and an adventure.

At another level it is mindfulness in practice. We escape our day-to-day existence, we centre ourselves, we are taken into a realm that is calm and focussed.

We contemplate the beauty of Country; we have an in-depth experience that takes us into our inner world. This is mindfulness. Our emotions are stimulated, fresh ways of thinking open up, and we enjoy simply being.

In addition, visual representations of Country have been going on in Australia for probably much longer than 65,000 years. They are part of an ancient tradition of art making in Australia.

This long and ancient tradition of being inspired by Country and painting Country has a shared history with the more recent European tradition of what is called *en plein air.*

Within this context I've shown how our perception of Country can be enriched by an understanding of the religious, and innate connection to and knowledge of land.

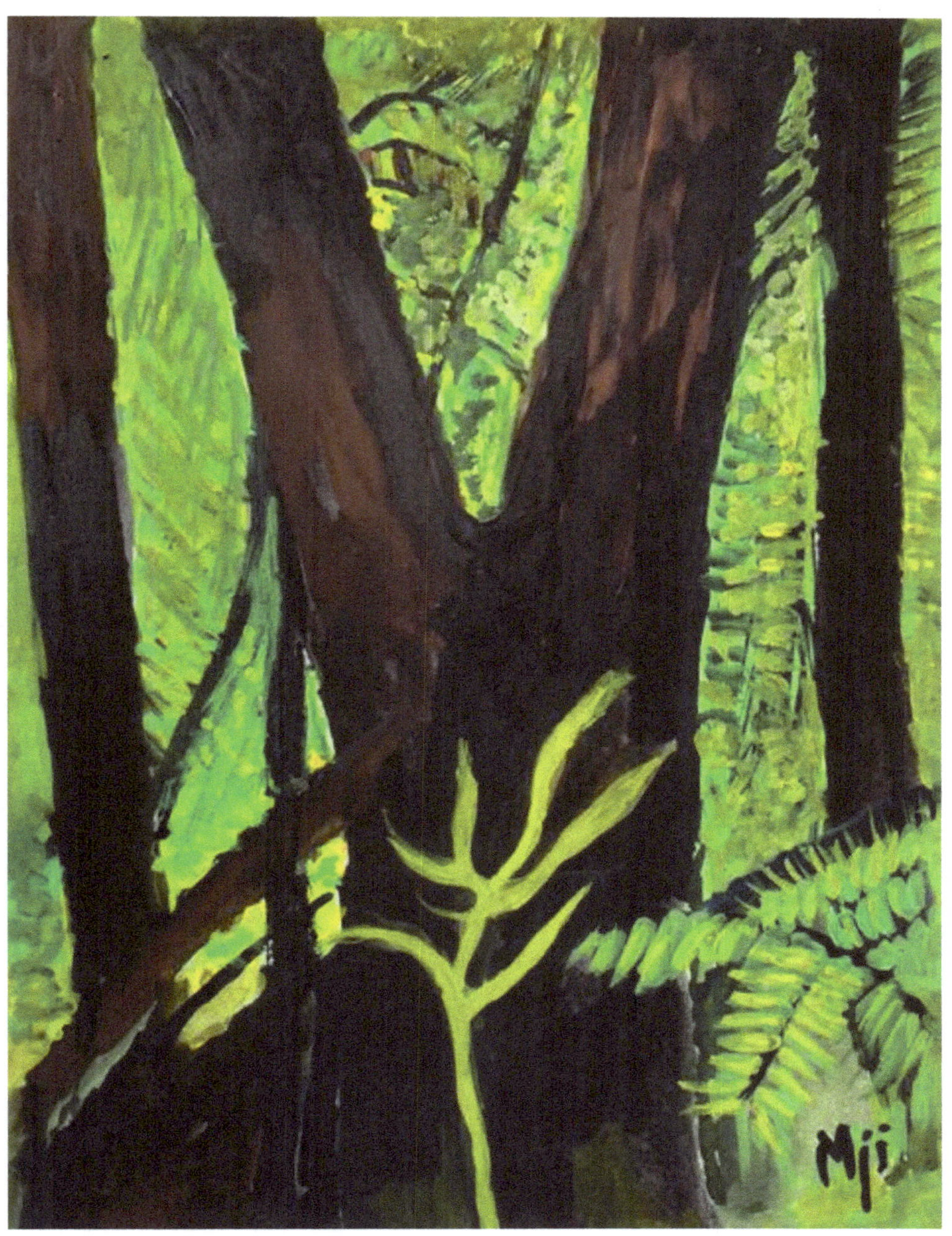

Back to Nature

About Marji Hill

Artist & Author

Marji Hill, a professional artist and painter since childhood, runs her art career alongside the writing of books.

Her art works range from very large oil paintings on canvas (her largest being 213 x 167cm) to very small works on paper - gouache being a favourite medium.

From these small paintings she makes greeting cards.

Marji's large oil paintings explore themes connected to Australian history and the Australian landscape. Black/white relations in Australia, reconciliation, Eureka, and the discovery of gold are common threads in her work.

Her small paintings are simple responses to land and sea environments.

Painting has been a lifetime passion for Marji. She remembers as a child winning first prize for a painting she exhibited at, was then, the Southport agricultural show. Then in her teens for two years in a row she won the Sunday Mail Child Art Competition in Queensland with her winning paintings getting full coverage in colour in the newspaper.

Marji's formal art training took place in the 1980s at the Canberra School of Art which in 1992 became ANU School of Art & Design.

As soon as she completed her Master of Arts Degree in Anthropology at the ANU, Marji went on to get a Post Graduate Diploma in Painting at the art school.

She has held eight solo exhibitions in Canberra, Melbourne and Sydney and has participated in various group shows.

One of her large paintings was included in the 2004-2005 Ballarat Fine Art Gallery's Traveling Exhibition *Eureka Revisited: the Contest of Memories*. This exhibition travelled to Melbourne, Canberra and Ballarat - part of the 150-year celebration of the Eureka Stockade.

Two of her large paintings were commissioned by the Citigold Corporation. One did hang for many years in the foyer of Jupiters Casino in Townsville until the casino was sold, becoming the The Ville Resort-Casino.

Jupiters Lucky Strike celebrates the discovery of gold by Indigenous boy, Jupiter Mosman in 1871 at Charters Towers. This painting today hangs in the offices of the Citigold Corporation in Charters Towers. The other, a portrait of Jupiter Mosman resides in the World Centre in Charters Towers in North Queensland.

Marji's paintings are in many private collections both in Australia and overseas and she is represented in the Ballarat Fine Art Gallery and Ballarat and Sydney campuses of the Australian Catholic University.

Alongside her art Marji has been writing books to promote understanding between Indigenous and Non-Indigenous Australians. She fostered the spirit of reconciliation in all her work since she was Research Fellow in Education at the Australian Institute of Aboriginal and Torres Strait Islander Studies (AIATSIS) in Canberra.

From 2008 to 2011, Marji was Deputy Chairperson of the Mosman Branch of Reconciliation Australia in Sydney.

Following her research fellowship at AIATSIS in 1976 Marji, together with her late partner, Alex Barlow, produced more than sixty-five books on all aspects of Aboriginal Australia including the critical, annotated bibliography *Black Australia*.

In 1989 Marji was the Project Coordinator and one of the researchers and writers of *Australian Aboriginal Culture* the official Australian Government publication on Aboriginal Australians and Torres Strait Islanders.

In 1988 her work of non-fiction *Six Australian Battlefields*, which she co-authored with Al Grassby, was published by Angus and Robertson. A decade later it was re-published by Allen & Unwin as a paperback edition.

Her nine-volume encyclopaedia, *Macmillan Encyclopaedia of Australia's Aboriginal Peoples* was published in 2000 and in 2009 she published *The Apology: Saying Sorry To The Stolen Generations*.

As part of her professional work, Marji travelled extensively throughout Aboriginal Australia and the Torres Strait.

Lucy Hauenschild

> Her maternal grandmother, Lucy Hauenschild, was an early Australian pioneer travelling as a small child with her family by wagon train from Melbourne to the Gulf Country in North Queensland.

> Her early years were spent with Aboriginal people around her and after leaving Croydon in the early 1900s she eventually in the early 1900s went to live and marry on Thursday Island in the Torres Strait.

> Lucy and her family eventually moved to the Gold Coast in the 1930s where she established *Ludoma* Hospital in Cavill Avenue at Surfers Paradise.

Following Marji's call back to her county, she returned to her birth place and now resides in Surfers Paradise pursuing her interests of writing, painting, mentoring self-publishing, and internet marketing.

Resources

Books

Australian Dictionary of Biography
http://adb.anu.edu.au/biography/namatjira-albert-elea-11217

Barlow, Alex 1994 *Australian Aboriginal Religions.* South Melbourne, Vic, Macmillan.

Barlow, Alex 1991 Tonanga: Albert Namatjira An Arrernte Man. South Melbourne, Vic., Macmillan. (Headliners)

Barlow, Alex & Hill, Marji 1997 *Art Of Arnhem Land.* South Melbourne, Vic, Macmillan. (Aboriginal Art)

Barlow, Alex and Hill, Marji 2003 *Indigenous Heroes and Leaders.* Port Melbourne, Vic, Heinemann Library.

Barlow, Alex & Hill, Marji 1987 *The Land and the Dreaming: Aboriginal Religions.* South Melbourne, Vic, Macmillan.

Barlow, Alex and Hill, Marji 2000 *The Macmillan Encyclopedia Australia's Aboriginal Peoples.* South Yarra, Vic, Macmillan.

Barlow, Alex & Hill, Marji 1997 *Rock Art*. South Melbourne, Vic, Macmillan. (Aboriginal Art)

Bell, Diane 1993 *Daughters of the Dreaming* St Leonards, NSW, Allen & Unwin.

Grassby, Al & Hill, Marji 1988 *Six Australian Battlefields*. Sydney, Angus & Robertson.

WEB RESOURCES

Camplin, Troy 2021 "Art as a Meditation Space" <https://medium.com/conscious-paradoxalism/art-as-a-meditation-space-3060ae99e1b7 "Art as a Meditation Space">

Fischer, Mary 2017 "Gouache vs Watercolor vs Acrylic: Do You Know the Difference?" < https://createlet.com/gouache-paint-vs-watercolor-paint-vs-acrylic-paint/>

Jenkins, Matilda 2017 "Plein Air Painting: What, When, Why, How and Who?" < https://bluethumb.com.au/blog/art-styles/plein-air-painting-what-when-how-why-and-who/environment >

National Gallery of Victoria 2021 < https://www.ngv.vic.gov.au/wp-content/uploads/2021/03/AUS_IMPRESSIONISM_LEARNING_RESOURCE_FA.pdf>

Qld Government. Department of Environment and Science. < https://parks.des.qld.gov.au/management/managed-areas/world-heritage-areas/current/gondwana-rainforests >

Qld Government. Department of Environment and Science. < https://parks.des.qld.gov.au/parks/springbrook/about/culture >

DOCUMENTARY

Back To Nature hosted by Aaron Pederson and Holly Ringland, ABC iView

More Books by Marji Hill

Self-improvement

Hill, Marji 2014 *Staying Young Growing Old.* Broadbeach, Qld, The Prison Tree Press.

Hill, Marji 2020 *How Big Is Your Why? An Author's Guide to Time Management and Productivity to Achieve Transformational Results.* Broadbeach, Qld, The Prison Tree Press.

Hill, Marji 2020 *A Create and Publish Toolbox: 101 Prompts In A Guided Journal To Help You Write, Self-publish, And Market Your Book On Amazon.* Broadbeach, Qld, The Prison Tree Press.

Indigenous Australia

Hill, Marji 2021 *First People Then And Now: Introducing Indigenous Australians.* 2nd ed. Broadbeach, Qld, The Prison Tree Press.

Hill, Marji 2021 *Australian Aboriginal History: 5 Stories of Indigenous Heroes.* Broadbeach, Qld, The Prison Tree Press.